Food Security in Africa

Edited by Barakat Mahmoud

Published in London, United Kingdom

IntechOpen

Supporting open minds since 2005

Food Security in Africa
http://dx.doi.org/10.5772/intechopen.77894
Edited by Barakat Mahmoud

Contributors
Bukelwa Grwambi, Nokuthula Vilakazi, Kumbukani Nyirenda, Emmanuel Vellemu, Yiseyon Sunday Hosu, Lubabalo Qamata, Mahamat Kabirou Dodo, Samkelisiwe Nosipho Hlophe-Ginindza, N.S. Mpandeli, Michael N.I. Lokuruka

First published in London, United Kingdom, 2021 by IntechOpen
IntechOpen is the global imprint of INTECHOPEN LIMITED, registered in England and Wales, registration number: 11086078, 5 Princes Gate Court, London, SW7 2QJ, United Kingdom
Printed in Croatia

British Library Cataloguing-in-Publication Data
A catalogue record for this book is available from the British Library

Additional hard and PDF copies can be obtained from orders@intechopen.com

Food Security in Africa
Edited by Barakat Mahmoud
p. cm.
Print ISBN 978-1-78985-733-7
Online ISBN 978-1-78985-734-4
eBook (PDF) ISBN 978-1-83962-166-6

For EU product safety concerns:
IN TECH d.o.o., Prolaz Marije Krucifikse Kozulić 3, 51000 Rijeka, Croatia, info@intechopen.com or visit our website at intechopen.com.

Meet the editor

Dr. Mahmoud is an international food safety expert with 30 years of experience in food safety. He was an Associate Professor in the Department of Food Science, Nutrition and Health Promotion at MSU. Prior to that, he held a postdoctoral position (in Food Safety) at Purdue University. He earned his Ph.D. in Marine Biosciences (Food Safety) from Hokkaido University (Japan). Prior to that he was a Visiting Scientist at the University of Lisbon (Portugal). He held a researcher position at the NRC (Egypt) between 1994 and 2000. He received his BSc/MSc degrees in Agricultural Sciences from Cairo University. The main goal of Dr. Mahmoud's work is to protect public health, reduce the prevalence of foodborne illness and promote the introduction of safer food using novel technologies. Dr. Mahmoud received more than $1M from the USDA, States and Food Industry to support his research (between 2008 and 2016). Dr. Mahmoud published about 100 publications (in international journals and/or conferences), two book chapters and edited a book entitled 'Salmonella-A Dangerous Foodborne Pathogen" (His publications have been cited more than 1200 times). He served as an editor-in-chief, editor/editorial board member for several international journals including Food Microbiology, Journal of Food Protection, Foodborne Pathogens & Disease, and African Journal of Food Science. Dr. Mahmoud has provided technical assistance in food safety in several developing countries in Africa, Asia, Central America, Middle East, and the Caribbean including Egypt, Malawi, Mozambique, Lebanon, Guatemala, the Dominican Republic, etc.

Contents

Preface

This edited volume is a collection of reviewed and relevant research chapters concerning the developments within the 'Food Security in Africa' field of study. The book includes scholarly contributions by various authors and it has been edited by a group of experts in food safety and availability, water issues, farming and nutrition. Each contribution comes as a separate chapter complete in itself but directly related to the book's topics and objectives.

The book consists of seven chapters that cover the topics: "Understanding Africa's Food Security Challenges" written by Dr. Mahamat Kabirou Dodo; "Regime Switch and Effect on Per Capita Food Security Issues in South Africa" by Drs. Yiseyon Hosu and Lubabalo Qamata; "Unlocking Water Issues Towards Food Security in Africa" by Drs. Nokuthula Vilakazi, Emmanuel Vellemu and Kumbukani Nyirenda; "Food Safety and Food Security in the Informal Sector" written by Ms. Bukelwa Grwambi; "The Role of Small-Scale Farmers in Ensuring Food Security in Africa" by Drs. Samkelisiwe Nosipho Hlophe-Ginindza and N.S. Mpandeli; "Food and Nutrition Security in East Africa (Rwanda, Burundi and South Sudan): Status, Challenges and Prospects" and "Food and Nutrition Security in East Africa (Kenya, Uganda and Tanzania): Status, Challenges and Prospects" both written by Dr. Michael N.I. Lokuruka.

The target audience comprises scholars and specialists in the field.

IntechOpen

Chapter 1

Understanding Africa's Food Security Challenges

Mahamat Kabirou Dodo

Abstract

Africa, sub-Saharan Africa (SSA) in particular, has for more than 10 years recorded a steady economic growth since the advent of the new millennium. Yet, despite this stellar economic growth, it faces challenges such as rapid population growth, persistent economic inequality, climate change threats, droughts, youth unemployment, undernourishment, and food insecurity. Understanding the state of food security in Africa, and addressing the above-mentioned challenges, should be the highest priority for Africa's Political Leadership. Not doing so will forever make Africa fail to achieve a sustainable economic development and create an inclusive shared-prosperity for its people. The African Union (AU), as well as respective national governments and regional organizations, and the international community at large, have in recent decades launched a multitude of policy initiatives aimed at addressing and tackling Africa's food insecurity and nutrition challenges. Despite those efforts and commitments by the disparate stakeholders, much remains to be done. This chapter presents Africa's food security and nutrition challenges, and sheds light on the climate change threats and potential consequences of the rapid population growth on Africa's food security. The chapter concludes with policy recommendations and proposals and makes points about Africa's bright prospects if food security were to be achieved.

Keywords: Africa, food security, climate change, population growth, economic development

1. Introduction

1.1 Africa since the end of the cold war

Since the end of the Cold War and the dissolution of the former Union of Soviet Socialist Republic (USSR) in 1991, Africa as a region has undergone a major structural transformation in social, political, demographic, and economic spheres. In political sphere, the region has gone from a one-party state governance to a multiparty democratic system ([1], p. 300). In social sphere, social governance is slowly but steadily being shared by the rising civil society and the NGOs that have now become copartners at addressing and debating social, economic, and political challenges in Africa. In demographic sphere, the region has seen a twofold increase in its population growth in the last quarter century. And finally, as regards to the economic sphere, whether voluntarily or involuntarily, since the 1990s, Africa has become a full participant in the economic and commercial globalization spurred by the West and led by the United States. And because of the abovementioned structural transformation of the continent, the region has nonetheless grown economically and registered stellar economic numbers in the last decades or so. That is, through the decade of the 2000s to the year 2013, for instance, the global boom in commodity prices propelled natural resources and oil- and gas-exporting African countries to register incredible economic growth and empower Africa into the twenty-first-century global economy [2]. As a result, Africa as a region is now a full member of the world economy and a coveted actor in the international economic arena.

However, despite the impressive recorded economic growth mainly by the energy and commodity-exporting African countries as stated above, as a region, Africa is still facing serious local and transnational challenges such as *youth unemployment*, *climate change threats*, *rapid population growth*, *undernourishment*, *domestic terrorism*, *drug trafficking*, *maritime piracy*, *protracted political crises and low-intensity short-lived wars*, and *conflict-induced famines* like the one we are witnessing in South Sudan today. Consequently, those challenges stand in the way against Africa's pursuit to achieve food security and eradicate hunger.[1] Therefore, if these above-cited challenges are not properly addressed and seriously tackled by the *African political leadership*, it is probably fair to say that achieving food security and meeting nutrition needs and targets as established by the Millennium Development Goals (MDGs) (2000–2015) and Sustainable Development Goals (SDGs) (2015–2030) will simply be another elusive quest for Africa among many other policy objectives and goals. In addition, if that happens to be so, the continent will unfortunately continue to languish behind other regions of the world in socioeconomic and human developments.[2] And consequently, it will be nowhere near attaining the SDG goals and targets just as it failed to meet the past MDG goals and targets. As a case in point, despite its modest registered economic growth and well-intentioned international policy initiatives such as the cited MDGs and SDGs aimed at fighting hunger and overcoming nutrition deficits [4] among many other human and development policy objectives, only few African countries managed to meet the MDGs 1c [5]. With that being said, this chapter sets out to present the state of Africa's food insecurity and nutrition deficits and addresses the potential impacts of the above-cited challenges, widely regarded today as the real barriers against successful eradication of food hunger and achieving food security in sub-Saharan Africa.

2. Defining food security

In this chapter, we use the definition of food security as stated by the United Nations Food and Agriculture Organization (UNFAO). The FAO's definition is our guiding principle and upon which our analysis of Africa's food security challenges is based. The FAO defines food security as "When all people, at all times, have physical, social and economic access to sufficient, safe and nutritious food that

[1] Ibid.

[2] See [3]. It is shown in it that out of 189 countries, only Algeria and Tunisia ranked in the top 100. Whereas, the last 10 bottom countries in the ranking were all Africans. They are as follows: 180 Mozambique, 181 Liberia, 182 Mali, 183 Burkina Faso, 184 Sierra Leone, 185 Burundi, 186 Chad, 187 South Sudan, 188 the Central African Republic, and 189 Niger.

meets their dietary needs and food preferences for an active and healthy life [6]." Nonetheless, achieving food security however requires that:

1. Sufficient quantities of appropriate foods are consistently available.

2. Individuals have adequate incomes or other resources to purchase or barter for food.

3. Food is properly processed and stored.

4. Individuals have sound knowledge of nutrition and child care that they put to good use and have access to adequate health and sanitation services [7].

2.1 State of food security in Africa

To begin with, it is worth pointing out from the onset that food insecurity is a multidimensional problem. It is a problem that is linked to *healthcare*, *conflicts*, *policies*, *politics*, *leadership*, *strategic vision*, *trade and economic interests*, *agricultural production*, *food system*, *global food industry trade politics*, *and the environment* (*mother nature*). As an example, in the sphere of healthcare, one can see a direct link between food insecurity, malnutrition, and a global pandemic like the HIV/AIDS. That is to say, if a member of a given family, for instance, is affected by the AIDS epidemic, the family of that patient will automatically lose a breadwinner and financial income generator. That is, the person affected by the disease will no longer be able to engage in any remunerative physical activity whether for themselves or for a third party in order to earn a living. Consequently, he or she will financially no longer contribute to his or her family well-being since they will not be able to generate any income whatsoever. And if and when that situation were to occur, the family of the patient in question would begin to eat less. The body of the affected person will by then have become vulnerable and weak to engage in any remunerative activity. As a result, food insecurity will then have set in, and poverty trap will have taken over and affected everyone within that family.

At the time of writing this chapter, Africa's state of food insecurity relative to other regions of the world, except for West Asia, is troubling and non-promising. Hence, understanding and accepting this reality should be of a concern for all Africans regardless of their socioeconomic and political status. That is to say, this said reality should be of a concern for *the African political leadership*, *the mayors of mega African cities*,[3] *the NGOs*, *the civil society*, *the media*, *the farmers*, *the business community*, *the youth*, *the academia*, *the churches*, *the mosques and other faith-based organizations*, and the *consumer organizations* alike. And according to the FAO 2015 State of Food Insecurity in the World *IN BRIEF*, Africa scores poorly in all indicators regarding food security and nutrition targets. For example, in 2015, only 18 out of 54 African countries have reached the MDG 1C hunger target (Millennium Development Goals 1C).

Furthermore, two of the many reasons why food security keeps evading millions of Africans are the never-ending conflicts and incessant political instability on the continent. Often, in many sub-Saharan African countries, foods are available and

---

[3] Africa today has 10 cities with populations of 3 million or more. They are as follows: (1) Lagos, Nigeria, 9,000,000; (2) Kinshasa, DRC, 7,785,965; (3) Cairo, Egypt, 7734, 614; (4) Alexandria, Egypt, 3811, 516; (5) Abidjan, Ivory Coast, 3.677, 115; (6) Kano, Nigeria, 3626, 068; (7) Ibadan, Nigeria, 3,565,108; (8) Cape Town, South Africa, 3433, 441; (9) Casablanca, Morocco, 3,144,909; and (10) Durban, South Africa, 3, 120, 282. For further illustration, see [8].

plentiful but not accessible to everyone. Poor families, for example, disproportionately pay the brunt of conflicts and wars. Farmers cannot bring their staple crops to the markets because of the lack of security even if and when they wanted to do so. Put it simply, conflicts disrupt markets and affect development policies that are put in place to assist the neediest of the population. And as a consequence of conflicts and wars, food prices rise, and poor families and their children can no longer have access to healthy and balanced dietary foods (*utilization*). Conflicts make food production drop since no one will risk their lives to work in the fields and bring foods to the markets while killings are raging. In the Central African Republic, for instance, the short-lived war of 2013 and its aftermath caused a drastic reduction in food production (*availability*) and engendered the rise of food commodity prices (*accessibility*). In fact, poor families and anyone else who could not have access to the foods in the markets were simply forced to live in subsistence. Consequently, thousands of Central Africans became nutrition-challenged because whatever was available for them to eat was obviously not meeting their nutrition needs and targets. Furthermore, widespread insecurity across the entire country made it more difficult to import foods from the neighboring countries or even receive foods from aid donors and the international community (*stability*) for that matter. As a result, food insecurity, and in many instances, the lack of foods thereof, became the daily reality of untold Central African families. And additionally, this added existential threat exacerbated an already desperate and deteriorating economic condition caused by years of protracted conflicts and political and economic mismanagement [9].

2.2 Why is sub-Saharan Africa suffering from food insecurity?

There are a lot of reasons as to why Africa and sub-Saharan Africa in particular is suffering from food insecurity and failing to meet its nutrition needs and targets. Though it is true that one cannot put their fingers at one specific reason as for why food shortages, insecurity, and prevalence of malnutrition uninterruptedly afflict sub-Saharan Africa, one can however identify a number of failed internal economic policy tools and international policy prescriptions as the culprit or underlying causes of systemic food insecurity in Africa. That is to say, on the internal front, for example, fewer among many reasons as for why food insecurity has been chronic in many African countries are the following: (1) *the never-ending political instability and crises*; (2) *the short or long protracted civil conflicts and wars*; (3) *the endemic, persistent, and institutional corruption*; (4) *the misdirected economic policies and mismanagement*; (5) *the lack of committed political leadership*; (6) *the sheer neglect towards the farmers*; and (7) *the lack of clear financial and economic investment into the agricultural sector*. On the external front, however, economic policy prescriptions mainly written and formulated by the World Bank (WB) and the International Monetary Fund (IMF) in the 1970s, 1980s, and the latter part of the 1990s directed at the African countries made an already difficult economic situation worse. This is because the architects of the alluded policies advised sub-Saharan African governments and leaders to cut aid and slash subsidies to their farmers. The economic policy rationale was that African countries should pull the plug under their parastatals (government-owned enterprises) and let the markets take care of everything. In addition, respective African governments were told that Africa should privatize and liberalize their economic policies in order to align them with the prevailing international trade, investment, and economic principles. Those economic recipes were said to modernize Africa and speed up its incorporation into the liberal-based global market economy. Consequently, because of those policy prescriptions, African farmers lost income supports from their respective governments, and millions of low-income African families became victims of food insecurity and nutrition deficits. In essence, the IMF and the

World Bank, and to a certain extent the US Treasury Department promoting and owning the so-called *Washington Consensus*, should be held responsible for those failed policies. For, they were the ones that devised, concocted, and directed them. As a matter of fact, they actively promoted or better said imposed them upon weak and hopeless African governments. And in turn, hapless African leaders implemented the said policies without truly understanding their future potential consequences on the farmers and their societies at large ([10], pp. 369–370).

So, with the benefit of hindsight today, one can say that those *structural adjustment programs* (SAPs) as they were known then, and devised by the above-cited international institutions and encouraged by the US Treasury Department, contributed to the demise of many farmers in Africa. They exacerbated the food insecurity and the existing precarious economic plights of millions of African families. And with the passing years, it has now become clear to any astute observer of the recent history of the social and economic development of Africa that African leaders of that time were not wise enough to reject and outrightly oppose those policies [9]. Actually, in fairness, many of them heartily and readily adopted the said policies and imposed them on their beleaguered poor populations. In fact, soon after they did so, many African countries began to import foods in huge quantity. And unfortunately, this situation has now lingered for decades. And honestly, as of today, there is no end in sight as to when the recurring food shortages and massive food imports in sub-Sahara Africa will either abate, subside, or end altogether. And for that, African countries constantly face food shortages now despite all the good and well-intentioned policies of the international community, the African Union, and African countries themselves intended to address rampant food insecurity, eradicate hunger, and bring food security to millions of low-income African families. So, as a consequence of all that, sub-Saharan Africa today is heavily dependent on food imports than at any time in its history. And as a result of that, it is sadly subjecting millions of its populations to the mercy of foreigners, commodity speculators, foreign exchange fluctuations, food aid giving nations, and the geopolitics of global food trade [11]. In actuality, this is the state of Africa's food security today. And as a matter of fact, when one looks back at the genesis of this episode, one can say without a doubt that this unfortunate situation could have easily been avoided. That is to say, had the *African political leadership* shown true leadership, heavily invested in agricultural sector and adopted economic nationalist policies, the early food production crisis, and insecurity beginning in the early 1970s would have been dealt with more effectively. Indeed, past African governments could have substantially invested in food production, assisted the small farmers with more aid and subsidies, and created policy resilience that would have saved thousands of African lives and farmers. And this may have possibly transformed and modernized the entire African food production system. In short, had the political leaders displayed true political courage to undertake such policies as stated, and shown true care for their respective populations, the concerns about the potential socioeconomic catastrophe of the rapid population growth in Africa will not have been as alarming and challenging to us as they seem today. To say the least, Africa suffers from food insecurity today and has been suffering from it for so long simply because of the utter failure and lack of vision, political courage, and sound economic policies of the *African leaders* and *economic decision-makers* of all political and ideological stripes on the Continent.

2.3 Impacts of rapid population growth and urbanization on the food security in Africa

In 1990, Africa's population was 635 million people. And, in 2018, the population of Africa stood at 1.2 billion people (see **Figure 1** below). However, except for the oil exporting African countries (see **Table 1**), sub-Saharan Africa has, on average, grown a meager 1.1% GDP in the last quarter century [15]. Now, considering Africa's demographic explosion in the last two decades, this underperforming GDP per capita growth is not sustainable for its long-term economic transformation. And clearly it will not help it either to meet the needs of millions of its young people that are reaching working age and expected to enter the labor market [16] in great numbers every year till the year 2030. This somber forecast is in addition to the fact that Africa's population is projected to double by 2050 (see **Figure 2** and New African March 2019 Guest Commentary by Peter Estlin, the Lord Mayor of London). Therefore, these serious challenges and threats are to be factored into any discussion about Africa's long-term economic transformation. That is to say, every social, political, and economic actor in Africa should seriously ponder upon them and properly address these threats and challenges. As the youngest continent, Africa has tremendous challenges ahead of it. At the same time, it also has great opportunity to unlock its economic potential that will benefit hundreds of millions of its peoples. However, this can only be done if *African political leadership and economic decision-makers* unselfishly invest into the youth and give it access to quality health and education and skills of the twenty-first century. And assuming that that warning is heeded, a vibrant, healthy, and educated young population will undoubtedly take upon itself to resolve the issues of food insecurity and nutrition

Year	Population	Urban Population	World Population	Africa's Share of World Population
2019	1,320,038,716	541,028,160	7,714,576,923	17.10%
2018	1,287,920,518	523,004,491	7,632,819,325	16.90%
2017	1,256,268,025	505,429,407	7,550,262,101	16.60%
2016	1,225,080,510	488,296,186	7,466,964,280	16.40%
2015	1,194,369,908	471,602,315	7,383,008,820	17.20%
2010	1,049,446,344	394,940,213	6,958,169,159	16.00%
2005	924,757,708	330,741,711	6,542,159,383	15.00%
2000	817,566,004	278,769,840	6,145,006,989	14.20%
1995	722,921,961	236,904,267	5,751,474,416	13.60%
1990	634,567,044	196,923,274	5,330,943,460	13.00%
1985	552,796,228	158,900,967	4,873,781,796	12.40%
1980	480,012,209	127,772,173	4,458,411,534	11.80%
1975	417,898,074	102,894,484	4,079,087,198	11.30%
1970	366,458,929	82,640,484	3,700,577,650	11.00%
1965	322,470,634	40,962,571	3,339,592,688	10.60%
1960	285,142,006	53,044,540	3,033,212,527	10.30%

Figure 1.
Evolution of Africa's population 1960–2019 (Source: [12]).

Rank	Exporter	Crude Oil Export (US$)	% World Total
1	Nigeria	$ 43.6 billion	3.8%
2	Angola	$ 38.4 billion	3.4%
3	Libya	$ 26.7 billion	2.3%
4	Algeria	$ 17.5 billion	1.5%
5	Rep. of Congo	$ 7.7 billion	0.7%
6	Egypt	$ 5.4 billion	0.5%
7	Ghana	$ 5.2 billion	0.5%
8	Equatorial Guinea	$ 4.1 billion	0.4%
9	Gabon	$ 4 billion	0.4%
10	Cameroon	$ 1.7 billion	0,2%
11	South Sudan	$ 1,6 billion	0.1%
12	Chad	$ 1.5 billion	0.1%

Table 1.
Top 12 Africa's crude oil-exporting countries in 2018 (Source: [13, 14]).

Year	Population	Urban Population	Urban Population %	Africa's Share of World Pop.	World Population
2020	1,352,622,189	559,506,598	41.4 %	18.3 %	7,795,482,309
2025	1,522,250,093	658,813,697	43.3 %	19.5 %	8,185,613,757
2030	1,703,537,504	770,067,953	45.2 %	20.8 %	8,551,198,644
2035	1,896,703,697	893,399,441	47.1 %	21.3 %	8,892,701,940
2040	2,100,301,731	1,029,050,896	49.0 %	23.6 %	9,210,337,004
2045	2,311,561,326	1,177,787,243	51.0 %	25.1 %	9,504,209,572
2050	2,527,556,761	1,338,565,979	53.0 %	26.6 %	9,771,822,753

Figure 2.
Africa's population forecast 2020–2050 (Source: [12]).

deficits, among many other challenges. As a matter of fact, a great number of economic experts and development economists agree with this economic proposition. They claim that quality health and education are the only engines of economic development that will help unleash the African potential, create inclusive prosperity for all, and economically transform the continent. (For further comments on the subject, see New African March 2019 Guest Commentary by Bill and Melinda Gates).

Furthermore, *Africa's political leadership*, *youth*, and *civil society* shall all understand that without some sort of family planning, albeit a voluntary one, the rapid unplanned population growth will never make Africa be food and nutrition secure. Therefore, understanding this reality, and taking also into account the cultural and religious sensitivities of several African communities, *Africa's political leadership*, *and faith-based organizations* of all denominations, should not have any problems investing in women, youth, and young girls. That is to say, in doing so, they will be able to properly educate mothers and future mothers and common people about the consequences of food insecurity and nutrition deficits on the future of their well-being and for Africa as a whole. That's because an uncontrolled rapid population growth, alongside the climate change threats and its effects, will be a formidable challenge for Africa to overcome if African people are not implicated in seeking solutions for their problems and challenges themselves. In our view, not adopting this policy approach will render the search for Africa's meaningful economic transformation unattainable just as many other unfulfilled African economic dreams (beginning since the years of its political independence in the 1950s, 1960s, and 1970s). The said contemplated family planning could also be managed through community programs, school programs, and after church and mosque services programs. And by devising such social program plans, educating people in major cities and the rural areas to understand what is truly at stake, and encouraging them to participate into the programs, it will be safe to say that Africans will take upon themselves the transformation of their agricultural production and adopt policies that will help them achieve food security on their own. And as such, they will be able to meet their nutrition needs and targets in line with their burgeoning population growths.

2.4 Impacts of climate change threats and effects on food security in Africa

Climate change debates pit true believers of climate change against those that oppose it. They also confront those who are skeptical of its existence or outwardly deny it against those who are fervent believers in it. However, the debates about whether climate change exists or not are beyond the intended purpose of this chapter. In it, we base our analysis on the existence of the climate change threats and its effects as an added challenge to Africa's existing agriculture commodities' production, food security, and nutrition needs and targets. In fact, as of today, changes in rainfall, soil quality, weather patterns, and precipitations in many regions of Africa have become the drivers for the food challenges and insecurity in all regions of the continent. And as a result of all that, climate change threats, effects, and stress are now the multiplier for the multitude of the daily challenges that Africans face. Furthermore, it is worth recalling that many countries in the world recognize today that climate change impacts on the temperature, precipitation, and droughts on a given community adversely affect the food security of that community. And consequently, many members of the said affected community are forced to leave and migrate to other communities. That is so because adverse or abrupt climate conditions and threats stress an entire community. And more often than not, they push their younger members to mass migrate. In addition, negative effects of the climate change event like floods and droughts destroy the agricultural production capacity and inputs of the impacted community. So, as an example, communities that have experienced events like droughts and floods whether in the *Sahel*, the *Lake Chad Basin*, or *East African region* [17] have all seen themselves abandoning their homes and villages and moving to neighboring communities or urban cities where they have no adequate resources to help themselves cope with their new surroundings and adapt to their new-found challenges. Many members of the said displaced communities become victims of food insecurity themselves. That is because by abandoning their villages and towns and moving to the new ones, they compete for scarce resources such as water and other daily living amenities in order to survive. Moreover, their sheer presence in their new hometowns or cities swells the pockets of the already established urban poor and makes life more miserable for themselves and everyone else. In short, climate change impacts and its effects have become existential threats to vulnerable communities. And one of the visible effects of climate change today is that climate change impacts turn members of the climate-impacted communities into *climate refugees* within their new adopted communities.

2.5 Impacts of protracted crises and conflicts on food security in Africa

According to the Fund for Peace, in 2017, the three most fragile states in the world were in Africa. Those states were the Central African Republic (CAR), South Sudan, and Somalia [18]. And each one of them has now become fragile because of the protracted crises that have kept it unstable since the 1960s. In the case of the Central African Republic, the years of the trouble started in the 1960s. In the case of Somalia, the disintegration of its *state apparatus* and the advent of its successive social, political, and economic challenges came after the fall of the regime of Siad Barre in 1991. In the case of South Sudan, the country has been in political turmoil, standoff, low-intensity warfare since it gained its independence from the Republic of the Sudan in 2011. However, it is worth noting that those three cited-above countries are not the only fragile countries in Africa. There are many other African countries that are also fragile and politically unstable because of the protracted conflicts and never-ending political crises. This is in addition to other crippling challenges such as *governance deficiencies*, *corruption*, *decades-long underperforming economies*, *weak institutions*, *flagrant human rights violations*, *and living resources scarcity* that have kept them from creating an inclusive and shared prosperity for millions of their citizens.[4] Indeed, food insecurity and nutritional deficits and the

[4] See *Good Governance and Human Rights: Keys to Building A Society That Works for All* by Muhammad Yunus in [19].

lack of quality health and education are the direct results of the said never-ending challenges that Africa as a whole confronts ever since it gained its *political independence* from the former colonial powers.

In effect, the persistent lack of peace and security in many sub-Saharan African countries today, coupled with the never-ending political instabilities and crises, is mainly the underlying reasons why African countries seem incapable of tackling and overcoming existential challenges and threats such as food shortages and insecurity and widespread malnutrition on their own. As a case in point, since 2010, a number of *civil wars and political crises* have broken out in several African countries from Algeria all the way to Kenya. In addition, newer political instabilities and short-lived *civil wars* have also occurred or unfolded in places like the Lake Chad Basin, Nigeria (Boko Haram), Libya (the bloody ousting of Muammar Kaddafi and the ensuing civil war), Egypt, Tunisia, the Central African Republic (CAR), Kenya, Cameroon, Mali, Burkina Faso, Burundi, South Sudan, Algeria, and Sudan as of late [20]. Moreover, countries such the Democratic Republic of the Congo (DRC), Sudan, and Somalia where decades-long conflicts have weakened and rendered their respective governments inept and unable to assume the administration of their territorial security and come up with sound national economic management policies, transnational threats such as *terrorism*, *mass migration*, *pandemics such as Ebola and HIV/AIDS*, *and maritime piracy* consume and divert their meager state resources away. Because of all that, their depleted resources are never sufficient to help them successfully fight institutional corruptions, rein into drug trafficking, curb hunger and other social woes, and effectively run their day-to-day administrative affairs. And as a result of the said overwhelming challenges, food insecurity and nutrition challenges currently affect and threaten the lives of millions of South Sudanese, Central Africans, Somali, Nigerians, and million more Africans today. For further illustration of how many African countries are afflicted and overwhelmed by conflicts and protracted crises, and why food security challenges have become existential threats not just to one or two countries in Africa, see *Cases of countries affected by food insecurity and acute malnutrition stemming from protracted conflicts*, *crises*, *and political unrests* and **Table 2**.

2.6 Cases of countries affected by food insecurity and acute malnutrition stemming from protracted conflicts, crises, and political unrests

1. **Nigeria.** This country has been grappling with severe security threats from Boko Haram and ISIS West Africa (ISIS-WA). Consequently, these threats have caused massive internal displacement of the population in the northeast region of the country and made thousands of Nigerians domestic refugees. In addition to the displaced Nigerian citizens, thousands more refugees from Niger, Cameroon, Chad, and the Central African Republic have flocked into the region, and consequently swelled the overrun refugee camps and made matters worse for everyone involved in the camps. As a result, they all have become victims of food and nutrition insecurity.

2. **South Sudan.** Due to the clashes between the South Sudanese Government and armed opposition groups, millions of South Sudanese have become the largest displaced population in their own country and been made refugees in the neighboring countries. As a consequence, this situation has created a severe case of food insecurity and malnutrition challenges in South Sudan today.

3. **Somalia.** This country is another case in Africa where protracted conflicts since 1991 have made it impossible for the Somali population at large to escape

A. Countries/territories with a protracted crisis	B. Countries/territories affected by conflict	C. Countries/territories with a protracted crisis affected by conflict	D. Countries/territories in fragile situations affected by conflict
Burundi	Algeria	Burundi	Burundi
Central African Republic	Angola	Central African Republic	Central African Republic
Chad	Burundi	Chad	Chad
Democratic Republic of the Congo	Cameroon	Democratic Republic of the Congo	Côte d' Ivoire
Djibouti	Central African Republic	Eritrea	Democratic Republic of the Congo
Eritrea	Chad	Ethiopia	Eritrea
Ethiopia	Republic of the Congo	Liberia	Guinea-Bissau
Kenya	Côte d' Ivoire	Somalia	Liberia
Liberia	Democratic Republic of the Congo	South Sudan	Libya
Niger	Egypt	Sudan	Mali
Somalia	Eritrea		Sierra Leone
South Sudan	Ethiopia		Somalia
Sudan	Guinea-Bissau		South Sudan
Zimbabwe	Liberia		Sudan
	Libya		
	Mali		
	Nigeria		
	Rwanda		
	Senegal		
	Sierra Leone		
	Somalia		
	South Sudan		
	Sudan		
	Uganda		

Table 2.
African countries in protracted crises, conflicts, and fragile situations (Source: Data extracted and compiled from [21]).

from poverty, misery, and the never-ending threats and real cases of food insecurity and chronic malnutrition that have for years affected both the youth and general Somali population.

4. **The Central African Republic.** This country is the latest case of food insecurity and widespread malnutrition in Africa. This has been the case since the short-lived Civil War of 2013 and the ensuing political unrest, rebellion, and ongoing sectarian aggressions between the Christian and Muslim communities.

2.7 Collective engagements and responses of the international community to tackling food insecurity in Africa

The international community heretofore understood as international institutions; private sector; multinational and transnational corporations (MNCs and TNCs); civil society; private foundations such as *the Bill & Melinda Gates Foundation*, *the Clinton Foundation*, and NGOs; leading nations such as the United States, China, India, Russia, and Brazil; the Global South; the European Union (EU); and celebrities like George Clooney, Angelina Jolie, Madonna, Bono, and many others are all stakeholders in food security and hunger debates. However, the United Nations (UN) system has thus far been the leading multilateral institutional voice that addresses and shapes the policy debates and proposes policy prescriptions for the food insecurity and malnutrition challenges that Africa and other regions of the world face.

Within the United Nations system, however, the Food and Agriculture Organization (FAO) which was established as an intergovernmental body is the organization mandated to address the agricultural issues such as food security, nutrition, and malnutrition challenges of its member countries. And as an intergovernmental body, the FAO was formed to promote the "common welfare by furthering separate and collective action for the purpose of raising levels of nutrition and standards of living of the peoples under their respective jurisdictions; securing improvements in the efficiency of the production and distribution of all food and agricultural products; bettering the conditions of rural populations; and thus contributing towards an expanding world economy and ensuring humanity's freedom from hunger [22]."

Though the FAO has had the mandate to tackle agricultural issues and concerns of its member countries, from its inception, the governments of its member countries were primarily the major actors that formulated and addressed the issues of agriculture within the United Nations' system. However, since the end of the Cold War, other actors and stakeholders such as the NGOs, CSOs, and a multitude of transnational corporations have also become relevant actors in policy formulations addressing hunger, food issues, and nutrition security governance in Africa. This has especially been so since the establishment of the MDGs covering the year 2000–2015 and the SDGs in place from 2015 to 2030. Nevertheless, this proliferation of stakeholders and actors in food security governance that is now being shared among the UN agencies and the private sector, civil society, NGOs, and the concerned governments has led to an increase in collaboration and partnerships among all the stakeholders that address and formulate policies dealing with the food and nutrition challenges in Africa today. As an example, transnational corporations such as *Unilever* have now jumped into global threats issues such as world hunger and food security and malnutrition challenges. This is becoming common in corporate governance because leading global corporations have now realized that those aforementioned issues are global threats in nature and no longer local per se. And therefore, they affect everyone and every country in this age of economic, political, technological, and cultural globalization [23]. Furthermore, corporations such as *Unilever* and many others like it have also understood that addressing those issues as a company or private sector is actually adhering to social corporate responsibility which is increasingly aligned with the interests of a business in this globalized and interdependent world. In fact, this new *social-business* approach has become the new *modus operandi* of socially responsible companies everywhere in the world today. In other words, it's good business to be a global corporate citizen. In effect, big corporations and brand-name companies now understand that consumers want them to also be social citizens while pursuing their economic and business profits and interests [24]. And as a response to all these new developments, in 2013, the FAO published its new *strategic framework* with a new focus on "governance, creation of enabling environments, and policy support in member countries is the direct outcome of its adaptation and repositioning process." This new framework was conceived to officially help the FAO collaborate and share policy spaces with other actors and stakeholders in food and nutrition security governance in Africa [25] and anywhere else for that matter.

2.8 Africa's engagements and commitments to ending food insecurity and nutrition deficits

Africa's responses to the food security challenges can at best be summarized as ineffective and inefficient thus far, to say the least. However, since the advent of the new millennium and the food crisis of 2007–2008, there has been a somewhat sincere and renewed commitment by the African leaders, the African Union, the Regional Economic Communities, the national governments, civil society, private sector, and all the stakeholders in Africa in support of food security. This new-found engagement in food security challenges is aimed at supporting agricultural production, replacing the prevalence of undernourishment, eradicating hunger, achieving food security, and meeting nutrition needs and targets. This has been so since the 2008 food price hikes and the subsequent social unrest and disturbances that took place in several African capitals and shook the sitting governments of that time. As a result of those vivid developments, the national security implications of food and nutrition insecurity were in plain view for all to see. In addition, the increased awareness of climate change threats and the rising awareness of the unforeseeable consequences of the rapid population growth on the food production system and on the stability of the *state* made African leaders take note and entice them to initiate various national policies to support food and nutrition security. Soon thereafter, as a result of those political events, several respective African governments devised new policy strategies in line with their national economic policies in support to food production, transformation, and security. For example, countries like Ghana, Nigeria, and Kenya partner more now with the private sector and the civil society in administering and managing their food systems. They basically have shifted their schemes towards private-public partnerships and involved wider private sector(s) in their food production and transformation policies. In contrast, countries like Ethiopia, South Africa, Angola, and Mali have integrated more of their food policy programs in recent years as well. That is, they have aligned them with their national economic strategies to support their food production, combat their food shortages, and replace their prevalent malnutrition. Nevertheless, what remains to be accomplished to date is the transformation of the said renewed political commitments into concrete policy actions such as (1) a visible and sustainable high-level leadership and effective governance, (2) an increase in public-private partnerships (PPPs) and shared co-leadership in fighting against hunger and food insecurity, (3) a supportive and enabling environment by the sitting governments and their decision-makers, and (4) a comprehensive and clear policy approach with all stakeholders involved in support of food production and security. Furthermore, at the continental and regional levels, it is worth highlighting also that the leading voices in formulating policies to combat food insecurity and curb the nutrition challenges in recent decades have been *the African Union Commission* (AUC), *the NEPAD*, and *the Regional Economic Communities (RECs) such as ECOWAS in West Africa and ECCAS in Central Africa*.

3. Conclusions

The current state of food security and widespread malnutrition in Africa is not as ideal as Africans would like it to be. That is to say, as of today, a good number of African countries are food deficit and insecure. This has been so because food insecurity and widespread malnutrition as stated in this chapter are a multidimensional problem. Challenges that are directly tied to healthcare, misdirected policies and politics, trade and economic interests, weak institutions, failed leadership, and many other variables make it hard and difficult for many African countries to achieve food security. In addition to the internal causes previously discussed as of why a good number of sub-Saharan African countries are not food secure, the chapter also highlighted that there are also external reasons as for why sub-Saharan African countries have been struggling to secure foods for their respective populations and meet their nutrition needs and targets. The chief among those external reasons as discussed and analyzed were economic policy prescriptions that the World Bank and the IMF prescribed for Africa in the 1970s, 1980s, and the latter part of the 1990s. The said policies were devised to help Africa align its economic development policies and strategies with the market-based liberal principles and practices. And as previously explained, the economic conditions of those countries later showed that those policy prescriptions did not provide the intended and expected economic results. Instead, they worsened the food insecurity in Africa. That's because by advising and encouraging African governments to cut their aid, subsidies, and assistance to their farmers in the name of the market-based principles, food insecurity in sub-Saharan Africa worsened dramatically. Moreover, the chapter also acknowledged that, save the commodities and natural resources exporting African countries, the economic growth of the majority of African countries has not performed as expected either. That is, the GDP growth rates of many sub-Saharan African countries have not kept pace with their rapid respective population growths, especially the rapid urban population growth that many African countries have experienced in recent years. In addition to the mentioned economic policy challenges, new challenges such as climate change and its effects and the internal displacements and migrations pushed many sub-Saharan African countries to depend more on food imports and foreign aid. Consequently, in actuality, many of them are unable to feed their populations today, and food insecurity and malnutrition have become the daily staple of millions of their citizens. Last but not least, the food price hikes of 2008 and their direct political consequences thereof, namely, riots and protests in many African cities, also exposed in plain view the economic policy failures of the African countries to the whole world to see. The rioting and protests showed how inept and incompetent many African leaders had for years been in failing to provide food security to their low-income and respective vulnerable citizens. Also, one of the visible consequences of the failure of African leaders in food security management has thus far been the continuous rise of import food bills in Africa year after year [26–34], while agriculture dependence has remained high. In sum, the combined reasons as analyzed above are the real reasons why sub-Saharan African countries have for years seemed unable to eradicate hunger, achieve food security, and meet nutrition targets and needs for their people(s). In essence, this is fundamentally why African countries struggled to meet the MDGs targets (2000–2015) despite the assistance and resources granted to them by the international community. With that in mind, if recent history is any indication, sub-Saharan African countries are going to struggle again in order to meet a few targets of the SDGs (2015–2030). In summary, hopefully African leaders will prove their skeptics and all of us wrong this time around.

4. Policy recommendations

The diagnostics of Africa's food security and malnutrition challenges has been thoroughly examined in this chapter. The international community, the African Union and respective African governments and anyone else interested in the issues of food insecurity, climate change threats, and protracted conflicts and wars in Africa have all launched policies against food insecurity in Africa. However, in order for Africa as a whole to achieve food security and lower its dependence on food imports and aid, *African political leaders and economic decision-makers* will have to surmount in true sense each one of the challenges mentioned in this chapter. For as those challenges are extensively analyzed in this chapter, they have been shown to be the real culprit of Africa's never ending socioeconomic and political problems. For decades now, they have been the challenges that have crippled Africa and hijacked the well-being and welfare of its citizens. Below are the specific policy proposals that if implemented could contribute to help overcome the challenges of food insecurity and nutrition deficits and many other challenges that have kept Africa for years from meaningful economic transformations beneficial for all its citizens.

5. Policy proposals

1. **African political leadership and economic decision-makers** should strive to formulate economic development strategies that are inclusive and people-centered rather than *elites and upper middle-class cosmopolitan-driven*. That is to say, Africa needs inclusive shared prosperity and constructive policies focused on Africa's youth and women and solely addressed against the challenges of a population set to double by the year 2050. Employment and job creation policies ought to also be the top priority beyond anything else for the *African political leadership*. Those are the real challenges that Africa will be facing in the next coming decades.

2. **African political leadership and economic decision-makers** should make agriculture a strategic sector and provide African farmers with all kinds of assistance and aid regardless of how unpopular they may appear to the international community and economic experts, and how contrary they may be when evaluated against the market-based principles and policies. In addition, credit and insurance schemes for farmers should also be part of any economic development policy and strategy in any sub-Saharan African country if food security were to ever be achieved. Instituting smart credit and insurance schemes for farmers will inevitably help create robust financial resilience that will protect them from market uncertainty and shocks and keep them focused on food production. Furthermore, civil society organizations, producer organizations, and wider private sector alike should also be allowed to participate in and be part of any policy scheme devised to support food production, combat food insecurity, and curb nutrition deficits.

3. **African political leadership and economic decision-makers** should institute and establish social protection programs or food safety net in the likes of cash transfer programs whose objectives should solely be to promote food security and nutrition and provide quality healthcare and education for the youth and women in particular whether in urban centers or in the rural areas. The programs should also serve against food price shocks for low-income citizens that are vulnerable to the market prices' volatility. Distribution programs and food banks in every neighborhood, town, and city across sub-Saharan Africa should also be established and aggressively promoted while implicating Africans of higher economic and financial means in the programs. The unscathed and seemingly unconcerned wealthy African families should also be invited to co-own the schemes and programs since they are resource-blessed and better off than the majority of their fellow citizens. That is to say, whatever incentive in the likes of tax break or any other financial schemes that may be attractive to them should be on the table for them to consider. Simply put, well-to-do Africans should be reminded of the famous *African solidarity* and the responsibility that comes with it in assisting their less-blessed brethren.

4. **African political leadership and economic decision-makers** should make all kinds of efforts to increase investment in food production and processing and physical transportation infrastructure that will connect rural areas with the growing urban centers where food demands are concentrated. Modern food storage facilities should also be built around major cities and link them to the four geographical corners of the back country. And this can be achieved only if food transportation networks within the country and across the immediate subregions are modernized and resourced.

5. **African political leadership and economic decision-makers** should understand once for all that without a sustained political stability and zero tolerance of any sort of institutional or personal (family-induced) corruption, agricultural production and food relief efforts that are badly needed to combat hunger, decisively tackle food insecurity, and achieve the nutrition needs and targets in Africa will never be possible. Peace therefore should be at the center of any national policy and be made the highest priority if Africa does not want to forever be dependent on the *good will* of foreigners, continuously import foods, and forever beg for development aid and largesse.

Additional information

JEL Code: N57, Q1, Q5, F63

Author details

Mahamat Kabirou Dodo[1,2,3]

1 International Academy of Social Science, Miami, FL, USA

2 Center of Excellence, Institute of European Studies, University of California, Berkeley, CA, USA

3 Centre de Documentaciò Europea, Universitat de Valencia, Valencia, Spain

*Address all correspondence to: mahamatkd@gmail.com

References

[1] Harris JE. Africans and their History. 2nd Revised ed. New York: Penguin Group; 1972

[2] Collier P. The Future of Capitalism Facing the New Anxieties. New York: Harper Collins Publishers; 2018

[3] Human Development Indices and Indicators, 2018 Statistical Update. 2018. Available from: http://hdr.undp.org/en/2018-update. It is shown in it that out of 189 countries, only Algeria and Tunisia ranked in the top 100. Whereas, the last 10 bottom countries in the ranking were all Africans. They are as follows: 180 Mozambique; 181 Liberia; 182 Mali; 183 Burkina Faso; 184 Sierra Leone; 185 Burundi; 186 Chad; 187 South Sudan; 188 the Central African Republic; and 189 Niger

[4] Hickel J. The Divide Global Inequality from Conquest to Free Markets. New York: Norton & Company; 2018

[5] Food and Agriculture Organization of the United Nations. Wide difference between regions. In: 2015 State of Food Insecurity in the World. Rome, Italy: United Nations FAO; 2015. p. 3

[6] FAO Policy Brief Food Security, Issue 2. 2006. Available from: www.fao.org/fileadmin/template/faoitaly

[7] The Four Dimensions of Food Security in ©FAO. EC-FAO Food Security Programme. 2008. Available from: www.foodsec.org

[8] Africa today has 10 cities with populations of three million or more. They are as follows: 1) Lagos, Nigeria, 9,000,000; 2) Kinshasa, DRC, 7,785,965; 3) Cairo, Egypt, 7,734, 614; 4) Alexandria, Egypt, 3,811, 516; 5) Abidjan, Ivory Coast, 3.677, 115; 6) Kano, Nigeria, 3,626, 068; 7) Ibadan, Nigeria, 3,565,108; 8) Cape Town, South Africa, 3,433, 441; 9) Casablanca, Morocco, 3,144,909; 10) Durban, South Africa, 3, 120, 282. Available from: http://worldpopulationreview.com/cities-in-africa/

[9] Korten DC. When Corporation Rule the World. 2nd ed. Connecticut, USA/San Francisco, California, USA: Kumarian Press, Inc./Berrett Koehler Publishers Inc.; 2001

[10] Meredith M. The Fate of Africa: A History of the Continent Since Independence, Revised and Updated. New York: Public Affairs; 2011

[11] Global Food Security Index 2018. Building Resilience in the Face of Rising Food-Security Risks in the Economist Intelligence Unit; 2018. p. 6

[12] Worldometers. Available from: www.Worldometers.info

[13] The World Factbook. Langley, Virginia, USA: Central Intelligence Agency;

[14] http://www.worldstopexports.com/worlds-top-oil-exports-country/ [Accessed: 23 June 2019]

[15] Zamfir L. Africa's Economic Growth: Taking off or Slowing Down? Strasbourg, France: European Parliamentary Research Service; 2016

[16] Harnessing Africa's Youth Dividends: A New Approach for Large-Scale Job Creation. Washington, D.C., USA: Brookings Institution; 2019

[17] Mozambique City Devastated by Cyclone Idai Was Working to Fight Climate Change. Associated Press; 2019. Available from: weather.com

[18] Fragile States Index Annual Report 2017. Washington, D.C., USA: Fund for Peace; 2017

[19] Yunus M, Weber K. A World of Three Zeros: The New Economics of Zero Poverty, Zero Unemployment, and Zero Net Carbon Emissions. New York: Public Affairs; 2017

[20] Sub-Saharan Africa: Key Issues and U.S. Engagement in Congressional Research Service Report. 2018

[21] The State of Food Security and Nutrition in the World Building Resilience for Peace and Food Security. New York City, USA: UNICEF; 2017

[22] Preamble of FAO's Basic Texts. Available from: www.fao.org/docrep/meeting/022/K8024E.pdf

[23] Steger MB. Globalization: A Very Short Introduction. Oxford: Oxford University Press; 2013

[24] Brill S. Tailspin: The People and Forces Behind America's Fifty-Year Fall and those Fighting to Reverse It. New York: Alfred A. Knopf; 2018

[25] Page H. Global Governance and Food Security as Global Public Good. Hans Page. New York, USA: New York University Center on International Cooperation; 2013

[26] Schuttenhelm R. Climate & Agriculture 1: African Food Imports Increase, while Agricultural Dependence Stays High. Ultrecht, The Netherlands: Bits of Science; 2018. Available from: http://www.bitsofscience.org/african-food-imports-agriculture-dependence-7906/

[27] Bes D, Trias F. El Libro Prohibido de la Economía-lo que las Marcas, los Bancos, las Empresas, los Gobiernos, ... No Quieren Que Sepas. Barcelona: Espasa; 2015

[28] Xi Jin-Ping: The Governance of China II. Beijing, China: Foreign Languages Press; 2017

[29] Gordon JS. An Empire of Wealth: The Epic History of American Economic Power. New York: Harper Collins Publishers; 2004

[30] Gordon JS. An Empire of Wealth: The Epic History of American Power. New York: Harper Perennial; 2004

[31] de Sassara H. Centrafrique la Dérive Singulière. Paris: L' Harmattan; 2014

[32] KDI Korea Development Institute. From Despair to Hope: Economic Policymaking in Korea 1945–1979: A Memoir by Kim Chung-Yun, Korea. Namsejong-ro, Sejong-si, South Korea: Korea Development Institute; 2011

[33] Schmidt E, Cohen J. The New Digital Age-Transforming Nations, Businesses, And Our Lives. New York: Vintage Books; 2014

[34] World Bank. World Development Report 2008: Agriculture for Development. Washington, DC: World Bank; 2007

Chapter 2

Regime Switch and Effect on Per Capita Food Security Issues in South Africa

Sunday Yiseyon Hosu and Lubabalo Qamata

Abstract

This paper examines whether the food security situation in South Africa is sensitive to the past and present governance systems. The study was aimed at reviewing the performance of key indicators: per capita land utilization, price index and consumption of a major staple food commodity (maize) in the pre- and post-apartheid periods. It also aimed at validating the application of population growth and food advocacy theories on South African food security. Time series analysis involving variables such as per capital land cultivation, consumption/tons and price/tons of maize within the period of 1970 to 2010 was conducted. Threshold autoregressive model (TAR) approach was used to capture per capita food security status of South Africans and to monitor trends under apartheid and post-apartheid eras. We found that there is a declining trend in per capita land cultivation and mixed results of per capita consumption of maize. The study revealed that population growth in South Africa has not been harnessed and there is possibility of worsening food security in the country. The long-run effect between the variables was established. The study recommends per capita targeting policy strategies for the improvement of staple food production and dietary balancing to ensure sustainable food security.

Keywords: agriculture, maize, population targeting, threshold autoregressive model

1. Introduction

Food security has different dimensions and so has been defined by many authors from different angles [1]. However, food security is a situation that exists when all people, at all times, have physical, social and economic access to sufficient, safe and nutritious food that meets their dietary needs and food preference for an active and healthy life is globally accepted [2].

Estimates show that out of 7.3 billion people in the world, approximately 795 million people or 1 in 9 were suffering from chronic undernourishment in 2014–2016 [3]. Almost all the hungry people, 780 million, live in developing countries, representing 12.9%, or 1 in 8, of the population of developing countries. Some 232 million people in Africa struggle with undernourishment daily [4]. This figure is about 29.3% of the total undernourished population and approximately 21% of the continent's population. Among all the regions of the world, sub-Saharan Africa is the only region that recorded a 10% (17.4–27.8%) increase in the number of hungry people between the periods of 1990–1992 and 2014–2016. Currently, 220 million people in sub-Saharan suffers hunger daily [4].

The continued population growth in Africa has rendered the per capita domestically grown food unchanged despite some improvements in agriculture with the resultant persistent hunger and poverty [5]. Although there has been tremendous growth in food production leading to a dramatic decrease in the proportion of the world's people that are hungry in the past decades, global food security situation still indicates that more than one out of seven people today still do not have access to sufficient protein and energy from their diet and even more suffer from some form of micronutrient malnourishment [6]. With the fastest population growth rate, Africa's population is projected to grow from about 796 million in 2005 to 1.8 billion by 2050 [7]. Despite urban migration, the number of rural dwellers will also continue to grow [8]. However, there are projections that parts of Africa, Asia and Central and Southern America will experience substantial declines in per capita cereal production if yields continue to grow slowly than per capita harvested areas [9]. Per capita food production in Africa declined by almost 20% between 1970 and 2000 [10].

Agriculture in African countries is widely seen to have performed worse than in Asia and Latin America. Production data per capita (of the total population) indicate that the amount of food grown on the continent per person rose slowly in the 1960s, then fell from the mid-1970s and has recently just recovered to the level of 1960 [5]. Comparatively, per capita food production increased by 102% in Asia and 63% in Latin America during the same period [5]. Studies have identified reduced investment in agricultural research, extension services and production systems by both the government and donor agents as the reasons for this [11–14]. Africa derives about 25% of its GDP from agriculture which provides jobs for 70% of the labour force, as well as a livelihood for more than 65% of the population [8]. It is however important to note that the level of local agricultural production will be determined by the amount and quality of arable land, the amount and quality of agricultural inputs (fertilizer, seeds, pesticides, etc.) as well as farm-related technology, practices and policies [9].

Interestingly, while some countries in Africa have witnessed growth in production [15], it has not necessarily improved the household food security status in the continent. South Africa produces enough food to feed its population; however, the country is increasingly experiencing worsening household food insecurity [16]. Despite the rise in employment in the country [17] and introduction of social grants by the government [18], the country has known little respite in terms of household food insecurity. About 35% of South African's population (14.3 people) experience hunger and undernutrition of which the majority are women and children [19]. Issues of ever-increasing food prices, lack of access to production resources and increased cost of electricity and oil prices are expected to make many more becoming food-insecure in South Africa [20, 21].

South African per capita land cultivation cannot be separated from the past dichotomous land ownership during the apartheid era where the white had ample access to land due to several discriminatory policies [22]. Effectively, many households in the so-called rural areas were and remain landless, while many others were left with tiny amounts of land. There are a few local black farmers that have private tenure of certain areas. Despite the abolition of the former homeland systems and subsequent redistribution of several commercial farms to emerging black farmers through leasing, access of other villagers to these lands for cultivation or collection of resources has been restricted under this arrangement [23].

South Africa is believed to have enough food supplies at a national level adequate to feed the entire population. However, a number of studies have revealed

DOI: http://dx.doi.org/10.5772/intechopen.86931

evidence of undernutrition among certain segments of the population [24]. There are evidence of undernutrition among certain segments of the population [25]. Inadequate nutrient intakes are often caused by household food insecurity, defined as a household's lack of access to amounts of food of the right quality to satisfy the dietary needs of all its members throughout the year [26]. Similarly, land requirements for food are determined by the production system, e.g. yields per hectare and efficiency in the food industry, which are also the resultant of consumption patterns [27].

1.1 Theoretical framework/theory underpinning the study

This study is underpinned by the Malthusian theory advanced by Thomas Malthus (1806) and the theory of food sovereignty promoted during the recent food crises of the 2007–2008 period. Malthusian theory is characterized by the views that there are too many mouths chasing too few calories as the population increases, lack of capacity to meet our food needs due to significant structural constraints, water and land degradation, distributional conflicts, and widespread, chronic food insecurity. Malthus in his prediction failed to conceive the development of important variables such as birth control and technology advancement in Agriculture. Although Malthus's theory promulgated in more than 220 years ago has been proven to be wrong, the question in the developing nation is how this growing population can be harnessed to produce enough food for all the population. The food sovereignty theory, unlike the Malthusian theory, believes that population growth is not the problem but the over-bearing power of international trade systems. Proponents of national food sovereignty movements generally favor agricultural policies that promote domestic production as an alternative to reliance on food imports. The theory of food sovereignty was first mentioned in 1996 when it became obvious that the global food organizations have no idea on how to ensure a food-secured world. Since then, the idea has gained prominence most especially in South America. Proponents of food sovereignty believe that all people have a right to healthy and culturally produced food through sustainable methods with local farmers having control over their own agricultural system [28]. The activists of food sovereignty are rallying cry against global agribusiness that stifles livelihood of smallholder farmers [29]. Food sovereignty theory rejects dependence on heavy chemical input for crop production that breed disparity in food access in the midst of growing food production [30]. It revolves around the concept of prioritizing local and household producers with opportunity of fair prices with the emphasis of community having control over productive resources like water, land and seed [31–33]. This theory believes that if they strive for a food-secured world, most go beyond the definition of the food security that revolved around sustenance of global food stock through international trade but do everything to empower the community with the right to produce for themselves rather than depending on the international market [29].

Finally, the trajectories by both theories speak to household food security and form a strong basis for analyzing per capita food status in South Africa. Although the Malthusian theory leans towards the far right on the outstripping tendencies of population growth based on limited resources, the theory of food sovereignty went too far to the left by opposing improved inputs most especially the chemicals and having nothing to do with international trade system. Considering the duality and capital-intensive agricultural sector of South Africa, a balanced food sovereignty theory will not only lead to local economic growth; it will also help engage the youthful population into productive farming activities, thereby improving per capita food security in South Africa.

Since the democratic dispensation in 1994, South Africa has undergone immense policy interventions aimed at improving the production capacity and food security situation of the citizenry. One of these policies, the Integrated Food Security Strategy (IFSS), was targeted mainly at increasing access to productive assets, including credit; increasing access to technologies, including food processing; supporting agriculture extension services; and improving infrastructure and trade regulations [34]. Another policy action, the Comprehensive Agriculture Support Programme, aimed at providing post-settlement support to the targeted beneficiaries of land reform and to other producers who have acquired land through private means and are engaged in value-adding enterprises for the domestic or export markets [35]. The programme was developed to benefit the hungry, subsistence and household food producers, farmers and agricultural macro-systems in the consumer environment. However, all these good policies have not really achieved the desired post-apartheid South African dream as the country's Human Development Index is ranked 118 among 135 countries and Human Poverty of 13.4% and ranking of 85 amidst all policies and strategies of improving the agriculture and food security (Global Food Security Index) [36].

This paper seeks to explore three main questions of South African food security systems. These questions are: is South African food security status sensitive to the past and the present governance regimes? Is the nationally acclaimed food sufficiency reflected in the household level? What effect does population growth in South Africa have on the food security status, is it positive or negative? These research questions are expected to generate inherent information on food security situations among South African households during the past apartheid era and the current black-dominated governance systems. This paper is set to determine per capita food security situation among South Africa households during the apartheid and post-apartheid eras. Specifically, the study seeks to determine the trend in per capita land cultivated, the price index and consumption level of maize staple foods. Various approaches have been followed to assess the world food situation. These include the development of large econometric models or the computation of technical indicators such as the population carrying capacity of the planet [37]. Within the South African context, many studies have focussed on food security status with different methodologies [20, 38, 39]; among others is a study that presents a policy impact analysis of South African food security [34]. However, this paper explores a new route, a simple-time series indicator approach. We used the indicator approach to capture food security status because it aids the process of monitoring trends and provides practical decision-making processes for enhanced policy-making processes and intervention strategies to cater for the most vulnerable individuals. We build on the theory of population growth as well as the food sovereignty theory for the comparison of per capita food security situation in apartheid and post-apartheid eras of South Africa. The analysis was undertaken to provide macro level trend information on the three main indicators: per capita land access, per capita staple food production and per capita consumption of staple food during the two important eras of South Africa. The insight and knowledge generated will be required for future policies formulation and interventions towards achieving sustainable food systems and security in South Africa.

2. Methodology

This study falls under post-positivism paradigm which believes that there is an empirical reality but that our understanding of it is limited by its complexity and by the biases and other limitations of researchers who conduct such research. Post-positivism holds that the goal of science is to achieve intersubjective agreement among researchers about the nature of reality rather than rely on the objective reality perceive through methods. In essence, issues should be viewed through the contributions of community of researchers rather than any individual researcher. Therefore, to address the research question, a quantitative approach was undertaken involving a time series data analysis. Similar to the approach by the FAO and USDA, a series data on Food Availability (Per Capita) Data System (FADS) include three distinct indicators which are land cultivated, price per ton and total food consumed of the selected staple food (maize). The study uses the threshold autoregressive model which is a nonlinear approach of representing time series data as suggested by practitioners who describe the basic proponents of the model [40].

2.1 Data collection

Secondary (times series) data on Production of the main staple food crops were sourced from National Agricultural Marketing Council (NAMC) from the period of 1970 to 2010. This paper focused on maize as the main staple food in South Africa. We believe the data are viable and reliable because NAMC is established by acts; it is recognized to offer advice to the government on food and trade issues. The data covered land cultivation, total production and consumption of these food crops. Corresponding national population for the same period (1970–2010) was also obtained from NAMC. It is worthy to note that the study was limited to the available and complete data on food commodity.

We undertake series data to determine food and dietary intakes of South Africans because it provides a pattern of food and dietary evolution over time, as a result of many factors and complex interactions. The factors are historical political change, income, prices, individual preferences and beliefs, cultural traditions as well as geographical, environmental, social and economic factors which all interact in a complex manner to shape dietary consumption patterns. Data on the national availability of the main food commodities provide a valuable insight into diets and their evolution over time [41].

2.2 Data analysis

Per capita land cultivation (ha), price index per tonne and capita consumption per tonne of the selected food crops were estimated by dividing total land cultivated and total consumption by the total population of South Africa. The percentage change in these food security indicators was also calculated to determine whether there have been positive or negative changes over the period under analysis.

The estimation of past and present (1970–2010) South African food security indicators for the selected staple foods was done through the equations below similar to the one used by the FAO:

$$PLCi\ (t) = TArabi\ (t)/Tpop(t) \tag{1}$$

where PLC is the per capita land cultivated of commodity i at time (t), $TArab$ is the total arable land of commodity i at time (t) and $Tpop$ is the total population at time (t).

The equation is expanded and modified into a multivariate regression by including the following explanatory variables that affect cultivated per capita land, namely, consumption per tonne and price index of maize. The regression is as follows:

$$LCUL\_CAP_t = \beta_0 + \beta_1 PRCE_t + \beta_2 CONSUMPTION_t + \varepsilon_t \quad (2)$$

where $LLCUL\_CAP_t$ is the ratio of the per capita land cultivated of the maize divided by the total population which is the dependent variable, $PRCE_t$ represents the price index of maize, $CONSUMPTION_t$ is the consumption per tonne of maize and $\mathcal{E}_t$ is the residual value for the regression. The TAR model in the following regression equation was adapted from a nonlinear approach study [42] based on Turkey's debt distress status [41]. The equation therefore for the purposes of the study is inscribed with threshold variables as price per tonne and consumption per tonne, with the dependent variable as per capita land cultivated:

$$\Delta y_t = \theta'_1 x_{t-1} 1_{(Z_{t-1} < \lambda)} prce + consumption + \theta'_2 x_{t-1} 1_{(Z_{t-1} \geq \lambda)} prce + consumption + e_t \quad (3)$$

where $x_{t-1} = \left(y_{t-1} r'_t \Delta B_{t-1}, \ldots, \Delta y_{t-k}\right)'$, and Z_{t-1} is the threshold variable per capita land cultivated of the maize to the total population which is the dependent variable ratio (LCUL_CAP) and includes explanatory variables, PRCE and CONSUMPTION for $t = 1, \ldots, T$, e_t is an iid error and $1_{(.)}$ is the Heaviside indicator function represented as follows:

$$1_{(.)} = \begin{cases} 1 & if \ Z_{t-1} < \lambda \\ 0 & if \ Z_{t-1} \geq \lambda \end{cases} \quad (4)$$

The threshold λ is given as unknown; this means the values in the interval $\lambda \in \Lambda = [\lambda_1, \lambda_2]$ where both threshold values are observed so that $P(Z_t \leq \lambda_1) = \pi_1 > 0$ and $P(Z_t \leq \lambda_2) = \pi_2 < 1$; the specification of the threshold variable Z_{t-1} assists as a framework of analysis of results that the variable is predetermined, strictly stationary and ergodic with a continuous distribution function [40].

The vectors θ_1 and θ_2 are distinguished according to specific components and are discussed as follows:

$$\theta_1 = \begin{pmatrix} \rho_1 \\ \beta_1 \\ \alpha_1 \end{pmatrix}, \ \theta_2 = \begin{pmatrix} \rho_2 \\ \beta_2 \\ \alpha_2 \end{pmatrix} \quad (5)$$

With scalar quantities represented by $\rho_1$and ρ_2 as the slope coefficients on y_{t-1}, β_1 and β_2 which have the same dimensions as r_t represent the slope on the deterministic components, α_1 and α_2 are the slope coefficients on $\left(\Delta y_{t-1}, \ldots\ldots, \Delta y_{t-k}\right)$ for the observed regimes.

The threshold estimates of the model are carried out with the use of least squares technique (more specifically, in this study we use the Huber-White covariance method in order to adjust the variance–covariance matrix of a fit from least squares, for heteroscedasticity and correlated responses). Each of the threshold value intervals $\lambda \in \Lambda$ is estimated by least squares (LS) as follows:

$$\Delta y_t = \hat{\theta}_1(\lambda)' x_{t-1} 1_{(Z_{t-1} < \lambda)} prce + consumption + \hat{\theta}_2(\lambda)' x_{t-1} 1_{(Z_{t-1} \geq \lambda)} prce + consumption + \hat{e}_t(\lambda) \quad (6)$$

where we let $\hat{\sigma}^2(\lambda) = T^{-1}\sum_1^T \hat{e}_t(\lambda)^2$ be the LS estimate of σ^2 for a fixed λ. The threshold estimate of the threshold value is found by minimizing $\sigma^2(\boldsymbol{\lambda})$ which are represented as

$$\hat{\lambda} = \underset{\lambda \in \Lambda}{argmin}\, \hat{\sigma}^2(\boldsymbol{\lambda})$$

To find the least squares estimates of other parameters, a point estimate $\hat{\lambda}$ is used in relation to.

$\hat{\theta}_1 = \hat{\theta}_1(\hat{\lambda})$ and $\hat{\theta}_2 = \hat{\theta}_2(\hat{\lambda})$; thus the least squares estimated threshold model is as follows:

$$\Delta y_t = \hat{\theta}'_1 x_{t-1} 1_{(Z_{t-1} < \hat{\lambda})} prce + consumption + \hat{\theta}'_2 x_{t-1} 1_{(Z_{t-1} \geq \hat{\lambda})} gsr + prce + consumption + \hat{e}_t \tag{7}$$

Eq. (7) shows the least squares residuals $\hat{e}_t$ and denotes the residual variance from the least squares estimation as $\hat{\sigma}^2 = T^{-1}\sum_{t=1}^T \hat{e}_t^2$, this equation is used in this study to draw standard Wald statistics and t-statistic inferences on parameters from Eq. (3) which can test the possible presence of nonlinearity.

Threshold effects

This examination utilizes the Wald test measurement to address the subject of whether the parameters of condition (3) have the nearness of limit impacts and the likelihood of general nonlinearity. This strategy is utilized in application to help the investigation of nonlinear time arrangement [40]. The limit impact vanishes under the joint theory where

$$H_0 : \theta_1 = \theta_2 \tag{8}$$

Condition (8), is a limitation that is tested through the observation of the standard Wald test written as: $W_T = T\left(\frac{\hat{\sigma}_0^2}{\hat{\sigma}^2} - 1\right)$; with $\hat{\sigma}^2$; speaking to the leftover difference from condition (6) and $\hat{\sigma}_0^2$ characterized as the remaining change from OLS estimation in condition (7) of the edge model. The dismissal of the invalid theory in condition (8) implies that there is factual importance of the logical factors of the model and that edge impacts exist.

Unit root test, asymmetry and cointegration

To test for stationarity, the test statistics are observed for the parameters ρ_1 and ρ_2 since they control the stationarity process of y_t in Eq. (3); as such, the null hypothesis is represented as follows:

$$H_0 : \rho_1 = \rho_2 = 0 \tag{9}$$

Eq. (3) is then rewritten as a stationary threshold autoregression in the variable Δy_t also implying y_t is $I(1)$ and therefore has a unit root.

Moreover, in a situation where $p = 1$, the model becomes stationary if $\rho_1 < 0, \rho_2 > 0$ and $(1 + \rho_1)(1 + \rho_2) < 1$. Hence this suggests an alternative to H_0 represented as $H_1 : \rho_1 < 0$ and $\rho_2 < 0$.

Unit root test can also be observed in a partial case where the alternative hypothesis reads as:

$$H_2 : \begin{cases} \rho_1 < 0 \ \ \underline{and}\ \rho_2 = 0, \\ \rho_1 = 0 \ \ or \ \ \rho_2 < 0. \end{cases}$$

Given that H_2 holds, then y_t will be observed as a unit root process in a single regime and a stationary process in another regime. Thus, in this case, a nonstationary process is observed, which is not a classic unit root process.

2.2.1 Augmented Dickey-Fuller (ADF) test

The ADF is the improved expansion of the condemned DF methodology and in that capacity is improved by including the slacked estimations of the reliant variable ΔY_t. The ADF test comprises of assessing the relapse as pursues [43]:

$$\Delta Y_t = \beta_1 + \beta_2 + \delta y_{t-1} + \sum_{i=t}^{m} \propto_i \Delta y_{t-1} + \varepsilon_t \qquad (10)$$

where ε_t represents the pure white noise term, $\Delta y_{t-1} = (y_{t-1} - y_{t-2})$, which shows the number of lagged differences which are often determined empirically. ADF also tests whether the unit δ is equal to zero and thus largely determines the trend stationarity and nonstationarity.

2.2.2 Phillips-Perron test

The Phillips-Perron (PP) test is a non-parametric methodology with the thought of disturbance parameters and consequently takes into account heterogeneous information circulation and pitifully subordinate factors [44]. The test is depicted to be increasingly vigorous regarding unspecified sequential relationship and heteroscedasticity in the model. Other studies legitimize the utilization of non-parametric test with regard to ordinariness suspicions being disregarded and affirm that non-parametric test like the Phillips-Perron test does not accept symmetry or any fundamental conveyance and is considerably more productive and incredible than parametric techniques [45].

The regression for the PP test as proposed by Phillips and Perron is represented as follows:

$$y_t = \alpha + \rho y_{t-1} + e_t \qquad (11)$$

where e_t is the Heaviside pointer I(0) and takes into account heteroscedasticity and all things considered the PP test revises for sequential connection and heteroscedasticity mistakes in e_t. The test insights under this model are appeared as $t_{p=0}$ and $T_{\hat{p}}$ which are changed and communicated as Z_t and Z_p measurements.

2.2.3 When threshold is unknown

For this situation, asymptotic conveyance is tried when there is no edge impact, implying that the limit esteem is obscure and hence the p esteems are additionally obscure for the given parameters. This is as indicated by hypothesis 5 by [40] where $\theta_1 = \theta_2$; therefore, $(t_1, t_2) \Rightarrow (t_1(u*), t_2(u*))$ and $R_T \Rightarrow R(t_1(u*), t_2(u*)) \leq \sup_{u \in [\pi_1 \pi_2]} R(t_1(u), t_2(u))$ where $u* = \underset{u \in [\pi_1, \pi_2]}{argmax}\, T(u)$.

This means that t-statistics are distributed by the functions $t_1(u)$ and $t_2(u)$ at random argument u^*. The trimming range represented as $[\pi_1, \pi_2]$ is free from nuisance parameters. The simulation of Monte Carlo experiment critical values of the 5% significance level is approximated to 10,000 replications. In summary, when there is no threshold effect observed, then the threshold value λ is not identified, and thus $\hat{\lambda}$ will remain the random sample, causing R_T to be random.

An Enders and Siklos test for cointegration and edge alteration is utilized [46] and is an expansion of the Engle-Granger test in light of the fact that it shows great power and size property over the Johansen test which accepts symmetric change in long-run balance [47], while, actually, Enders and Siklos test catches the topsy-turvy nature of long-run equilibrium modifications.

2.2.4 When threshold is known

In the case where the threshold effect is observed, this means that a threshold value (λ_0) is identified and thus the parameters of Eq. (3) are not equal, $\theta_1 \neq \theta_2$; it is also assumed that $E\Delta y_t = 0$ which is observed in model (3) given that assumption 1 by Caner and Hansen which shows $\mu_1 P(Z_{t-1} < \lambda) + \mu_2 P(Z_{t-1} \geq \lambda) = 0$ holds. However if $E\Delta y_t \neq 0$, then a time trend is included in model (3), and Δy_t is replaced with $\Delta y_t - E\Delta y_t$; therefore, a long-run variance and long-run correlation are defined given that the Δy_t remains stationary and ergodic; hence, we let

$$\sigma_y^2 = \sum_{k=-\infty}^{\infty} E\left(\Delta y_t \Delta y_{t-k}\right) \tag{12}$$

According to Theorem 6 by Caner and Hansen, if the parameters from Eq. (3) are not equal, and if $E\Delta y_t = 0$ and the variance $\sigma_y^2 > 0$, then the t-statistic function is given as

$$-t_1 \Rightarrow \left(1-\delta_1^2\right)^{1/2} Z_1 + \delta_1 DF \ll DF \;\; and \;\; -t_2 \Rightarrow \left(1-\delta_2^2\right)^{1/2} Z_2 + \delta_2 DF \ll DF$$
$$Given\ that \begin{pmatrix} Z_1 \\ Z_2 \end{pmatrix} \sim N\left(\begin{pmatrix} 0 \\ 0 \end{pmatrix}, \begin{pmatrix} 1 & \sigma_{21} \\ \sigma_{21} & 1 \end{pmatrix}\right) \tag{13}$$

Along these lines, this is autonomous of the negative of the traditional without pattern Dickey-Fuller t-circulation. Additionally, the Dickey-Fuller gives a preservationist bound on asymptotic dispersion, yet in addition the two-sided Wald test measurement has a valuable articulation and bound which is accounted for under hypothesis 6. In outline, when an edge impact is watched, this implies λ is distinguished, and for extensive examples, λ will be close to the true value of the threshold λ_0; this means that the asymptotic distribution of R_T is similar to the case where the threshold value λ_0 is known.

The threshold adjustment for cointegration uses the Enders and Siklos test for a case when the threshold value is known. The null hypotheses $P_1 = 0$ and $P_2 = 0$ along with the joint hypothesis are $P_1 = P_2 = 0$, while t-Max is the maximum threshold with the largest test statistic, with F statistic denoted by ϕ, and thus the ϕ statistic can reflect a rejection of the null hypothesis $P_1 = P_2 = 0$ at the point when just a solitary one of the qualities is negative. In any case, on the off chance that both the p esteems are negative in measurement nature, at that point the invalid theory comes up short conceivable dismissal. Furthermore, the ϕ measurement rejects the invalid speculation of no cointegration at the 1% criticalness dimension, and t-Max measurement rejects the invalid theory at 5%, yet not the 1%, centrality level, in this manner inferring that the disseminations of ϕ and t-Max will rely upon test estimate and the quantity of factors incorporated into the cointegration relationship. Be that as it may, the outcome is controlled by the utilization of the Enders and Siklos test approach and Monte Carlo basic qualities that additionally depend on the dynamic idea of the threshold adjustment process.

3. Results and discussion

3.1 TAR model results

LLCUL_CAP is the threshold variable and is separated into two regimes with observations. The TAR model shows the threshold value for both regimes to be −2.09%, with the first regime consisting of 16 observations ($Z_{t-1} < \lambda$) and the second regime having 22 observations ($Z_{t-1} > \lambda$). The threshold level is negative in the analysis because arable land is a fixed asset that cannot be increased, while the South African population growth is increasing. The relationship between the threshold variables and the explanatory variables (price per ton and consumption per ton) is differentiated into the different regimes. In the first regime with 16 observations, the price per ton shows a coefficient of −0.1365 and carries a negatively related coefficient against the cultivated land/area, which means that an increase in LPRCE_TON has the effect of decreasing LLCUL_CAP (per capita maize-cultivated land) with a margin of 13.7%; this is shown in **Table 1**.

Consumption per ton (LCONSUPTION_TON) also carries a negatively related coefficient of −0.8236 against the threshold variable (cultivated land) which suggests that increases in consumption per ton put downwards production pressure on cultivated land area, with a margin of 82.4%. The denoted relationship therefore resulted in 16 observations that are less than the threshold value which suggests that during the pre-1994 apartheid era, the negative relationship was sustainable and did not go past the threshold level of −2.09%; in the first regime, the LPRCE_TON is not statistically significant with t-statistics and p-value that are above the 5% significance level, while LCONSUPTION_TON is reported to be statistically significant as p-values are less than 5%; this is shown in **Table 1**.

In the case of the second regime, both explanatory variables are statistically significant, with p-values that are below 5%. The threshold variable (cultivated land) has 22 observations that are below the threshold value indicating unsustainable per capita food security. The coefficient for both price per ton and consumption per ton is still negatively related in the regime, with LPRCE_TON shown as −0.265 and LCONSUPTION_TON as −0.6907. These values suggest that an increase in LPRCE_TON and LCONSUPTION_TON results in decreasing cultivated area/land of maize. The results suggest the cultivated land area of maize was not sustainable at the threshold value of −2.09% for food security and imply that the cultivated land area has diminished beyond the negative threshold value with at least 22 observations.

A more descriptive observation of the result is shown by **Figure 1** for actual, fitted and residual model for the transformed data. More specifically, attention is given to the actual and fitted model in the figure. As from 1970 to 1988, the first regime is observed, while the second regime continues from 1989 to 2010, where the first regime with 16 observations shows the cultivated land remains sustainable even though it negatively slopes and decreases. However, in the second regime, as located from 1989, the behaviour changes, because the actual and fitted models show a further decline in cultivated land area beyond the threshold value at 22 observations; this makes the second regime unsustainable.

The results of per capita consumption and the change in consumption trend over the period of analysis from 1970 to 2010 are indicated in **Figure 1**. The food security indicators (per capita land cultivated and per capita consumption) presented in **Figure 1** indicate the validity of food sovereignty theory with the evidence that

DOI: http://dx.doi.org/10.5772/intechopen.86931

	Threshold variables							
	LLCUL_CAP(−3) < −2.09 with 16 observations $Z_{t-1} < \lambda$ **(first regime)**				**LLCUL_CAP(−3) = > −2.09 with 22 observations** $Z_{t-1} > \lambda$ **(second regime)**			
	Coefficient	**Std. error**	**t-statistics**	**p-values**	**Coefficient**	**Std. error**	**t-statistics**	**p-values**
LPRCE_TON	−0.136533	0.085868	−1.590037	0.1214	−0.265049	0.042998	−6.164189	0.0000
LCONSUPTION_TON	−0.823665	0.280937	−2.931847	0.0061	−0.690729	0.257767	−2.679666	0.0114
	Non-threshold variable							
C	5.621432	2.146702	2.618636	0.0132				

Table 1.
TAR model estimates.

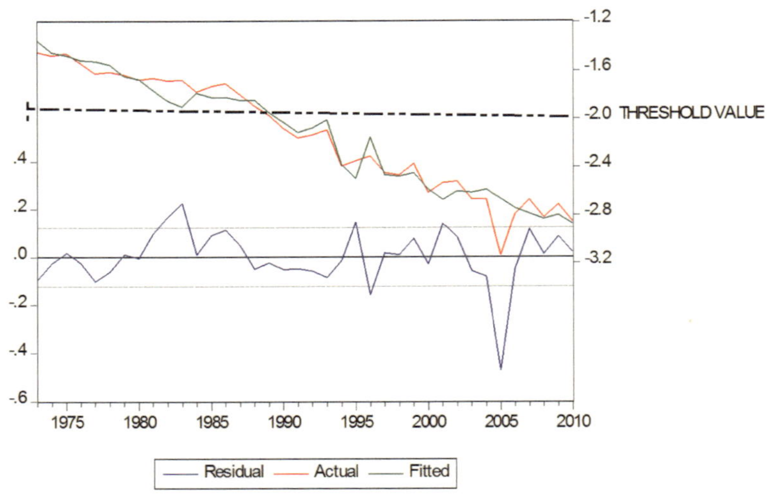

Figure 1.
Actual, fitted and residual models.

growth in income and productivity captured by gross domestic products (GDP) of South Africa has not necessarily translated to a food-secured country, and at the same time, the evidences that households have not been put to their optimum productivity in agriculture, hence the declined per capita food security within the household level. The dynamics of the past era coupled with interaction between increasing population growth, lack of employment, and food prices have really affected food security status of South African households. The increase in poverty and food insecurity in South Arica has opened up debate and focussed the attention of the governments and researchers towards the development of strategies that will rediscover issues on vital production such as land ownership, natural resources renewal and conservation and holistic revamping of support systems. In a similar study, a reported decline in land cultivated of staple foods in South Africa is a result of population growth, land use changes and reduction in yields per hectare [48]. Available evidence indicates that most African nations are facing increasing rural population densities and person-to-land ratios, as well as increasing agricultural labour force amidst decreasing area under crop cultivation [49].

Global and regional per capita decline has been projected [9]. However, it was estimated that per capita cereal production in Southern Africa will increase annually by 8% till 2030. Our analysis showed that maize per capita production has had a turbulent increase in the recent past with the tendency of dropping (**Figure 1**). Climate change and substantial water scarcity intensified by anthropogenic increases in air temperature and evaporation [50]. It is also expected that rapidly growing populations and increasing temperature will place further demands on scarce water supplies [51]. Biofuels and rising demand by the global middle class will probably compete for global production, raising prices and reducing food access for rural and urban poor.

3.2 Emerging themes

We have used time series data to analyze per capita food security involving three main indicators: land utilized for cultivation of maize, price index of maize and consumption of maize during the apartheid and post-apartheid eras of South Africa. Below are some emerging themes that came out of the analysis:

3.2.1 Diminishing returns and unharnessed growing population

The case of diminishing returns on productive resources, especially in the agricultural sector, was evident in the analysis. While this cannot be pinned to a specific factor due to the nature of the study, it suffices to say here that great attention must be paid to the environmental factors that surround agricultural resources such as land and water, most importantly in the face of the threatening global climate change. We also found that as the population grows, the per capita indicators declined. This shows that there are issues of unutilized segment of population and lays doubt on supporting systems to harness the population for productive works to avert the prediction of Thomas Malthus in South Africa as well as strengthen the involvement of household in national food security agenda.

Another factor that can explain this phenomenon is the lack of or slow assimilation of improved agricultural technology to enhance per capita yield of land. Although there are few large firms producing with improved technologies, their output is crowded out by the majority of small farming households that are not using improved technologies for an intensified agriculture.

3.2.2 Observed pressure of consumption and price of maize in both regime

The analysis showed that both tons of maize consumed and price per ton have had depressing impacts on per capita maize cultivation in both regimes. This speaks to maize price policy stability in South Africa mainly because prices for maize within the country are determined in international market. This can also be explained with the insensitivity of per capita maize cultivation to increase in consumption (demand). This can further be explained with lack of or low access to improved agricultural technologies among the growing South Africa populace which is a necessity for sustainable food security.

4. Conclusion

The aim of this study was to examine whether household food security situation in South Africa is regime sensitive by creating three basic food security indicators as well as validating the effect of population growth. We found that food security status in South Africa is regime insensitive because it has fallen below the threshold level in both regimes. However, the unsustainable food security observed in the apartheid era (noticed in 1987 thereabout) could be ascribed to political agitation for freedom from apartheid regime, sanctions and relocation of many white farmers. More importantly, the results also showed that post-apartheid policies and intervention actions involving land redistribution, expanded food production and security mostly targeting poor households have achieved little impact on their targets as the indicators showed reverse dire situations even with the regime changed and the country being led by black South Africans. Again, we attribute this to lack of access to new and improved agricultural technologies, not just access to land by many small farms in South Africa. In line with the findings of this study, the dire situation of lack of access to new and improved agricultural technologies can be improved when pragmatic land reform that will provide title documents to the majority of landless South Africans is achieved. This will serve as collateral and is expected to increase access to credit that is needed to acquire improved agricultural technologies and increase production frontiers. Another important factor is revamping access to agricultural extension services to the smallholder farmers as the case for precision agriculture increases for food security. Currently, there are only few white farmers that have access to quality agricultural extension services because they can pay for them.

Furthermore, the results showed that per capita land cultivation of maize has declined steeply in the post-apartheid era compared to the apartheid era. The situation showed that South Africa will be vulnerable to shock in the international markets and increase in price. There is no other important warning on food insecurity than this going by the fact that South Africa maize price is controlled by international market. Similarly, the result showed that the country has yet tapped on its increasing population as the per capita land cultivation of the important staple food are very low. South African land policies need to be readjusted to per capita land/productive resources targeting to improve food security. The percentage change in land cultivation showed the successes of agricultural policies are not sustainable.

Declining South Africa per capita agricultural output especially that of the staple foods is an indication that the country needs to expedite capacity building and readjust its agricultural internship programme to improve South African agricultural systems and household food security. There are indications that food value chain and franchise development in South Africa have affected the consumption pattern.

In relation to the theory of population growth and the food advocacy (theory of food sovereignty) for food security within South Africa, it is obvious that the population has grown, thanks to the innovations in birth control and child development, but it has not been harnessed to better food production. On the other hand, the depressing impacts of total consumption of maize and price per tons further indicate the exposure of South Africa food system to external factors which the proponents of food sovereignty are against. We recommend that agricultural policies should employ per capita targeting, revamp agricultural support systems, engage in aggressively improved agricultural technology transfer to empower domestic production systems and insulate smallholders from harsh international trade system in order to make South Africa a real food-secured nation.

Author details

Sunday Yiseyon Hosu* and Lubabalo Qamata
Department of Economic and Business Sciences, Walter Sisulu University, Mthatha, South Africa

*Address all correspondence to: drsyhosu@gmail.com

References

[1] Hoddinott J. Choosing Outcome Indicators of Household Food Security. Washington DC: IFPRI; 2001

[2] Food and Agricultural Organisation of United Nations (FAO). Feeding the World: Aggregate Agriculture. Rome: FAO; 2010

[3] Nord M. Introduction to Item Response Theory applied to Food Security Measurement: Basic Concepts, Parameters, and Statistics. Technical Paper, Rome. FAO; 2014

[4] FAO, IFAD and WFP. The State of Food Insecurity in the World 2015. Meeting the 2015 International Hunger Targets: Taking Stock of Uneven Progress. FAO: Rome; 2015

[5] Pretty J, Toulmin C, Williams S. Sustainable intensification in African agriculture. International Journal of Agricultural Sustainability. 2011;**9**(1): 5-24

[6] Godfray HCJ, Beddington JR, Crute IR, Haddad L, Lawrence D, Muir JF, et al. Food security: The challenge of feeding 9 billion people. Science. 2010; **327**:812-818

[7] United Nations. World Population to 2300. Department of Economic and Social Affairs/Population Division. New York: United Nations Secretariat. 2004;**254**

[8] Garrity DP, Akinnifesi FK, Ajayi OC, Weldesemayat SG, Mowo JG, Kalinganire A, et al. Evergreen agriculture: A robust approach to sustainable food security in Africa. Food Security. 2010;**2**:197-214. DOI: 10.1007/s12571-010-0070-7

[9] Funk CC, Brown ME. Declining global per capita agricultural production and warming oceans threaten food security. Food Security. 2009;**1**:271-289

[10] Abdulai A, Barret CB, Hazell P. Food aid for market development in sub-Saharan Africa. In: DSGD Discussion Paper No. 5. Washington, DC, USA: Development Strategy and Governance Division International Food Policy Research Institute (IFPRI); 2004. p. 56

[11] Department for International Development (DFID). Building Our Common Future in Sub-Saharan Africa. London: Department for International Development; 2009

[12] Eicher CK. Building African scientific capacity in food and agriculture. Review of Business and Economics Literature. 2009;**LIV**(3): 238-257

[13] Haggblade S, Hazell P, editors. Successes in African Agriculture: Lessons for the Future. Baltimore: Johns Hopkins University Press; 2009

[14] Roling N. Africa Can Feed the World, SR 16A, Foresight Global Food and Farming Project. London: Foresight Global Food and Farming Project; 2010

[15] Food and Agriculture Organisation Statistics (FAO). The State of Food Insecurity in the World. Addressing Food Insecurity in Protracted Crises. Rome: FAO; 2010

[16] Van der Berg S. In: Bhorat, Kanbur, editors. Poverty and Policy in Post-Apartheid South AfricaPublic spending and the poor since the transition to democracy. Pretoria: Human Sciences Research Council Press; 2006. pp. 201-231

[17] Aliber M. Exploring Statistics South Africa's national household surveys as sources of information about food security and subsistence agriculture. In: Unpublished Report, Centre for Poverty Employment and Growth. Pretoria,

South Africa: Human Sciences Research Council; 2009

[18] Abdu-Raheem KA, Worth SH. Household Food security in South Africa: Evaluating extension's paradigms relative to the current food security and development goals. South African Society of Agricultural Extension. 2011; **39**(2):91-103. ISSN 0301-603X

[19] Human Sciences Research Council (HSRC). Food Security in South Africa: Key Policy Issues for the Medium Term– Position Paper. Pretoria: Human Sciences Research Council; 2004

[20] Altman M, Hart TGB, Jacobs PT. Household food security status in South Africa. Agrekon. 2009;**48**(4):345-361

[21] Labadarios D et al. The Assessment of Food Insecurity in South Africa. Pretoria: Human Sciences Research Council; 2009

[22] Aliber M. Chronic poverty in South Africa: Incidence, causes and policies. World Development. 2003;**31**:473-490

[23] Shackleton CM, Shackleton SE. Household wealth status and natural resource use in the Kat River valley, South Africa. Ecological Economics. 2006;**57**:306-317

[24] Steyn NP, Abercrombie R, Labadarios D. Food security—An update for health professionals. South African Journal of Clinical Nutrition. 2001;**14**:98-102

[25] Vorster HH. The link between poverty and malnutrition: A South African perspective. Health SA Gesondheid. 2010;**15**(1):435-441. DOI: 10.4102/hsag.v15i1.435

[26] Charlton KE, Rose D. Prevalence of household food poverty in South Africa: Results from a large nationally representative survey. Public Health Nutrition. 2002;**5**(3):383-389

[27] Gerbens-Leenes PW, Nonhebel S, Ivens WPMF. A method to determine land requirements relating to food consumption patterns. Agriculture, Ecosystems and Environment. 2002;**90**: 47-58

[28] Patel R. Food sovereignty. Journal of Peasant Studies. 2009;**36**(3):663-706

[29] Alkon AH, Mares TM. Food sovereignty in US food movements: Radical visions and neoliberal constraints. Agriculture and Human Values. 2012;**29**(3):347-359

[30] Holt-Giménez E, Altieri MA. Agroecology, food sovereignty, and the new green revolution. Agroecology and Sustainable Food Systems. 2013;**37**(1): 90-102

[31] Beuchelt TD, Virchow D. Food sovereignty or the human right to adequate food: Which concept serves better as international development policy for global hunger and poverty reduction? Agriculture and Human Values. 2012;**29**:259-273

[32] Bello W. How to manufacture a global food crisis. Development. 2008; **51**(4):450-455

[33] Desmarais AA. The power of peasants: Reflections on the meanings of La Vía Campesina. Journal of Rural Studies. 2008;**24**:138-149

[34] Koch J. The Food Security Policy Context in South Africa. Brazil: International Policy for Inclusive Growth; 2012

[35] CASP 2003–2005. Comprehensive Agricultural Support Programme (CASP). Department: Agriculture Republic of South Africa

[36] Global Food Security Index. The Economist Intelligent Unit. New York: The Economist; 2015

[37] Irz X, Roe T. Can the world feed itself? Some insights from growth theory. Agrekon. 2000;**39**(4):513-528

[38] Baipethi M, Aliber M, Jacobs P. Agricultural employment scenarios. In: Hall R, editor. Another Countryside. Policy Options for Land and Agrarian Reform in South Africa. Cape Town: Institute for Poverty, Land and Agrarian Studies, University of the Western Cape; 2009. pp. 121-163

[39] Hendriks SL. The challenges facing empirical estimation of food (in) security in South Africa. Development Southern Africa. 2005;**22**(1):103-123

[40] Caner M, Hansen BE. Threshold Autoregression with a unit root. Econometrica. 2001;**69**(6):1555-1596

[41] WHO/FAO. Diet, nutrition and the prevention of chronic diseases. WHO Technical Report Series 916. Rome: WHO; 2003

[42] Yilanci V, Ozcan B. External debt sustainability of Turkey: A nonlinear approach. International Research Journal of Finance and Economics. Sakarya University. 2008;**20**:91-98

[43] Gujarati DN. Basic Econometrics. United States Military Academy, West Point: McGraw Hill. International Edition; 2003. ISBN: 0-070-112342-3

[44] Phillips PCB, Perron P. Testing for a unit root in time series regression. Biometrika. 1988;**75**(2):335-346. DOI: 10.2307/2336182

[45] Leybourne SJ, Newbold P. The behaviour of Dickey-Fuller and Phillips-Perron tests under the alternative hypothesis. The Econometric Journal. 1999;**2**(1):92-106

[46] Enders W, Siklos PL. Cointegration and threshold adjustment. Journal of Business and Economic statistics. 2001; **19**(2):166-176

[47] Engle RF, Granger CWJ. Co-integration and error correction: Representation, estimation, and testing. Econometrica. 1987;**55**(2):251-276

[48] Biggs R, Scholes RJ. Land cover change in South Africa 1911-1993. South African Journal of Sciences. 2002;**98**: 420-424

[49] Jayne TS, Yamano T, Weber MT, et al. Smallholder income and land distribution in Africa: Implications for poverty reduction strategies. Food Policy. 2003;**28**:253-275

[50] Parry ML, Canziani OF, Palutikof JP, Linden PJ, Hanson CE, editors. IPCC (2007) Climate Change 2007: Impacts, Adaptation and Vulnerability. Contribution of Working Group II to the Fourth Assessment Report of the Intergovernmental Panel on Climate Change. Cambridge: Cambridge University Press; 2007

[51] Hosu YS, Cishe EN, Luswazi NP. Vulnerability to climate change in the Eastern Cape Province of South Africa: What does the future hold for smallholder crop farmers? Agrekon. 2016. DOI: 10.1080/6803031853. 2016.1157025

Chapter 3

Unlocking Water Issues Towards Food Security in Africa

Nokuthula Vilakazi, Kumbukani Nyirenda and Emmanuel Vellemu

Abstract

Water plays an important role in food security and provides the basis for healthy ecosystems and human well-being. The relationship between water and food production is key to creating resilient and sustainable food systems. This chapter will discuss the effects of water quality and scarcity with respect to food security in Africa. The effects of water availability and its usage in the African landscape and how this has impacted food security will be highlighted. Lastly, issues concerning water pollution and food safety will be tackled to identify knowledge gaps that impede food security in Africa in its efforts toward attaining the United Nations Sustainable Development Goals.

Keywords: agriculture, availability, contaminants, ecosystems, food security, health, pollution, safety, sanitation, scarcity, water quality, water

1. Introduction

Water is an important resource that supports life on earth. Its availability plays key roles for attaining socio-economic developments globally [1]. It is also a priority toward meeting the United Nations Sustainable Development Goal (SDG) 6 that seeks to ensure access to water and sanitation for all [2]. This requires an adequate enabling environment and strong systems at country level. The United Nations General Assembly has called for country-led, coordinated efforts to provide financial resources and build capacity and technology transfer to help countries yield stronger and sustainable services [3]. Water is thus an essential resource for balancing the well-being of humans and healthy ecosystems.

The survival of humans and continuing social-economic developments depend on the supply of appropriate water quality and quantity. The relationship between humans and ecosystems is core as people strive to improve their well-being. Ecosystem services are beneficial to all living creatures including humans in a number of ways [4]. Water, for instance, contributes to ecological functions through the provisioning of habitat for aquatic life, including fish that is food for humans.

Water also provides ecosystem services that include freshwater supply, regulatory functions such as dilution and water purification, and fulfilling cultural necessities (e.g., water for traditional, esthetic, or medicinal and spiritual purposes). The benefits derived from ecosystem services are available to humans, regardless of where they live or where the services are generated. For example, urban dwellers enjoy river ecosystem service benefits including fishing for food or growing trees

 IntechOpen

along the river banks, which can be used as timber to build houses or as firewood for cooking.

Ensuring sustainable management of aquatic ecosystems for improved food security is therefore important [5]. This is especially true in urban areas where human activities may pollute distant ecosystems through effluent discharges caused by industrial and domestic or mining activities [6]. Human activities can pollute water bodies and impact socio-economic developments negatively. Any changes in water quality can affect short- or long-term food security goals if aquatic resources are not properly managed.

This chapter discusses the effects of water quality and scarcity with respect to food security on the African continent. A comprehensive synthetic evaluation of various published and technical reports was conducted in order to draw the relationship between the potential of water and food security in the African region. The use, distribution, and requirement for food systems that promote water conservation to create sustainable food production are explored. Lastly, issues concerning water pollution and food safety are discussed to identify knowledge gaps that impede food security in Africa toward the attainment of the United Nations Sustainable Development Goals.

2. Water and human survival

This section seeks to highlight the basic human need for water and track the global water distribution and its importance in food security. Water is a basic unit of life and an essential nutrient that is required in amounts that exceed the body's ability to produce it [7]. Like all nutrients, water performs different functions in the body [8]. Water is an essential component of cells, tissues, and organs required for digestion, absorption, and dissolution and as a carrier for nutrients, eliminating waste products; temperature regulation; and as a lubricant and shock absorber [9–11].

To achieve all these functions, total body water must be approximately 60% of body weight in males and 50% of body weight in females [12]. The water distribution is up to 60% intracellular (this amount is lower in females due to larger amounts of subcutaneous tissue and smaller muscle mass) and 20% in extracellular space [13]. The extracellular fluid compartment comprises fluid in blood, interstitial fluid, bone, connective tissue, and transcellular fluid. Variation in water intake depends on human health, weight, and human physical performance.

Human survival can be achieved with minimum water requirement where water lost through normal activities gets replenished [14]. The average adult body naturally loses almost 2–3 L of water daily which must be replenished to function on a day-to-day basis. This loss occurs mainly via urine, perspiration, feces, and exhaled air.

The amount of body water that gets lost depends on individual and environmental factors. These factors are affected by the climate a person lives in, his or her age, physical activity level, and kidney function [8]. To regulate the body's water levels, the water input must balance water output through metabolic processes (0.3 L/day), fluid intake triggered by thirst (1.5 L/day), and solid foods triggered by appetite (approximates 0.7 L/day). Too little or too much water in the body can lead to less-than-optimal body function.

Early stages of decreased water intake in the form of dehydration can lead to difficulty in concentrating, headache, and sleepiness. Decreased water intake has also been associated with bladder and lower urinary tract cancer and increased risk of colorectal cancer as well as kidney stone formation [15]. Taking too much water can also put an unnecessary burden on the cardiovascular system and the kidneys and can cause a drop in the concentration of electrolytes in cells causing harm in the long run.

While water may be a renewable resource, it is unfortunate that there is only a finite amount and there are no substitutes. Without clean and safe water, human survival cannot be achieved. This has a great impact on the global burden of disease, health, education, and economic productivity of populations.

2.1 Water challenges affecting human survival

Water is an important component in a number of human functions, hygiene, and the overall maintenance of health. At the most basic level, water service must meet consumption and hygiene needs and sustain good health at household level [16]. Millions of the world's poorest people, however, die each year from preventable diseases due to poor hygiene, lack of clean drinking water, and lack of proper sanitation facilities [17].

The reality is that water and sanitation are weakly integrated into countries' poverty reduction strategies. Many national governments are failing to put in place the policies and finances needed to accelerate progress toward achieving clean water and adequate sanitation.

In many rural communities, lakes, dams, and stream that are the main sources of water run dry for long periods, forcing people to use unsafe water sources [18]. For the 2.1 billion people who lack access to clean water, they can only afford to get a measly 5 L a day and fail to meet the recommended basic minimum of 20 L a day required for human health, economic, and social development [19]. This is a far cry from the 200 L a day per person that people from rich countries consume on average in a day.

A report on global distribution of the global drinking water services in 2015 found that 71% of the global population (5.2 billion people) had access to a safely managed drinking water service [19]. The report further found that sub-Saharan Africa was the region with the lowest number of people with access to safe drinking water located on their premises. Only Australia and New Zealand had 100% access, where all of the population had basic services (including basic drinking water, sanitation, and hygiene) in their households.

The same report estimated that two-third of the total global population was living in water-stressed areas that experience water scarcity for at least 1 month in a year in 2015 [2]. Of the two-third, 844 million people lacked basic drinking water service and 263 million people were reported to be spending over 30 minutes per round trip to collect water from an improved water source [19].

Still, 159 million people were reported to collect drinking water directly from surface water sources and over half of these people were living in sub-Saharan Africa. These people share their domestic water sources with animals. A large fraction of the people that live in extremely vulnerable situations of water scarcity all year-round are found in Libya, Somalia, Pakistan, Morocco, Niger, and Jordan where 50–90% of the country's population lives under those circumstances [20].

3. Global distribution of water

An estimated three fifth of the earth's surface is covered by water, which makes up a total volume of almost 35 million km^3 [2]. Of the available amount, only 200,000 km^3 (1%) of this is fresh water that is usable by humans. This is the water that is expected to fulfill the demands of the increasing global population, meet the food production needs using the limited amount of arable land, and sustain industrialization.

Historically, people looked for location to set up their livelihoods near water supplies such as river bases that could provide drinking water and carry off waste. Over time, areas close to water sources became populated by industries and agricultural holdings which use water for irrigation and also to power industries [21].

Distribution of piped water is realized as a sign of progress toward achieving the SDGs. Industrialized countries (20%) have managed to achieve piped water coverage in 85% of their entire household. The poor countries, however, have only managed limited piped water coverage with only 25% of all their households having access [19]. Industrialized countries have been better able to achieve water security compared to poor countries and this is evident from the average water usage data of 200 L per person per day in rich countries compared to the 5 L per person per day in poor countries [18].

Factors that contribute to high water scarcity levels include areas with a high population density, areas with irrigated agriculture, and areas with very low natural water availability [20]. Geographically, water scarcity can be found in in the world's arid areas with low water availability like the Sahara, Taklamakan, Gobi, and central Australian deserts.

Water scarcity has also been found to be intense in areas with high population density and irrigation intensity. Globally, these areas are found near river basins and include the Ganges basin in India, the Limpopo basin in Southern Africa, and the Murray-Darling basin in Australia [20].

Distribution by sectors shows that water use is spread between domestic, agriculture, and industry sectors. Agriculture accounts for over 70% of freshwater use [16, 22] and industry water use accounts for 20% globally. In spite of this, it is believed that there is enough water in the world for domestic, agriculture, and industry purposes; the only problem is how this water is distributed especially to the poor who are systematically excluded from the distribution.

Water use varies significantly by sector across the world. How do these three sectors use fresh water?

3.1 Agriculture

As discussed above, water use varies considerably across the world especially between the poor and rich. Agriculture is the biggest user of fresh water with Africa and Asia, accounting for the largest users under this sector with an estimated 85–90% of all freshwater [23]. Future demands for water for agriculture are threatened by climate change, technological development, and urbanization. The challenge is to produce more food to meet the growing population demands using less water and other resource inputs in an environmentally friendly manner [24]. Low-income countries' average agriculture usage is estimated at 90%; 79% for middle income and only 41% in high incomes countries [22].

3.2 Industry

Industrial water use includes all the water used for manufacturing, energy generation, and other industrial activities such as dilution, steam generation, washing, and cooling of manufacturing equipment [25]. Globally, an estimated 20% of total available fresh water is used for industrial purposes. Within the industrial sector, hydropower and nuclear power generation uses 57–69% and the thermal power generation uses 0.5–3% [23]. Industries also pose a threat to fresh water because of the amount of wastewater it produces, its mobility, and loading of industrial pollutants and their potential impacts on water resources, human health, and the environment. High-income countries tend to use the largest portion of water on industries (17%), with low-income countries using the least with an average 2% [26].

3.3 Domestic

Domestic water is the most visible form of water and it shows the problem that exists in the distribution of fresh water between the rich and the poor. People in developed countries consume almost up to 10 times more water daily than those in developing countries. In developed countries, where large cities have centralized water supply and an efficient canal system, domestic consumption averages 200 L per person per day [23].

In developing countries within Asia, Africa, and Latin America regions, consumption in cities and towns is between 50 and 100 L per person per day, and in the water scarce areas within these regions, the amounts can be as low as 5 L per person per day [23]. Countries with the largest population, China followed by India, have the highest water use globally [26].

The change in water distribution will have a serious implication on people's health and well-being, especially for people living in high population density areas, areas with irrigated agriculture, and areas with very low natural water availability. These are the estimated 1.8–2.9 billion people who experience severe water scarcity for at least 4–6 months per year and the 500 million people face severe water scarcity all year round [20].

The distribution of water between sectors is expected to change over the coming years as a result of population growth, increased water scarcity, and drought due to climate change. Water use for irrigation and other water using sectors of the economy are expected to experience extreme competition which will place more burden on food security.

4. Water in food security

Water forms an essential part in national food security. To attain food security, there must be an acceptable quantity and quality of water for health, livelihoods, ecosystems, and production [27, 28]. Any sustainable attainment of food safety and security for a fast-growing population requires thoughtful decisions to develop and manage water resources.

Food security and safety are key development agenda items in most developing regions (Global Panel on Agriculture and Food Systems for Nutrition, 2016). Global research and funding have been prioritized and channeled toward fighting against food insecurity. Although substantial progress globally is evident [29], the same cannot be said for some of the African regions. Sub-Saharan Africa continues to have less access to sufficient quantity and quality food for proper health and growth. The report also classified the sub-Saharan countries as food insecure, with limited access to safe food within their population.

Despite the global food security achievements realized in recent years, food security and limited access to food safety still remain as challenges in Africa. Water scarcity and irregular rainfall distribution are proving to be an impediment to Africa's efforts to ensure food security. Agriculture production systems, which are the backbone of food security, are also adjusting to tightening water availability by reducing freshwater use especially in the African region. This has resulted in the emergence of new diets that are sensitive to the significant influences of water and land use [30].

As the water challenge for agricultural production in Africa increases, it is expected that the share of irrigated agriculture in global water use could rise by over 30% by 2030 [30]. Total global water demand could double by 2050. The increased competition for scarce water and land resources increases concerns about where the additional food will come from. The challenges are further exacerbated by climatic changes that cause irregularities in water availability across the African landscape [31].

Water requirements in agriculture vary significantly not only in terms of quantity, but also in terms of quality and timing depending on food type. This is very significant especially when it comes to staple foods such as maize, rice, and wheat that are critical in food security of many countries in Africa. Some of these countries have increased awareness toward conserving their national water supply by opting for virtual water trade—importing food from outside the country in the effort to conserve water resources and maintain food security [32]. Other countries have shifted food production within the agriculture sector focusing more on planting water-efficient crops.

Apart from water being important in production, it also plays a huge role in food processing, transformation, and preparation adding to the competition against industrial and domestic water use [33]. Even though food processing uses much less water than primary production, this part of the food system requires water that is of high-quality standards and that does not pose any health and safety risks on both human and ecosystem health.

There is also a drive toward introducing water-use efficiency, reducing pollution impacts from processing industries [34]. Poor quality water used in food processing can lead to food-borne disease such as diarrhea and other diseases that contribute to malnutrition. The unsafe food creates a vicious circle of diseases affecting particularly the more vulnerable populations that include children, the elderly, and the sick [33].

Priority must be given to encouraging greater efficiency of water use and the development of integrated water management plans [30]. The shortage of food production due to water scarcity calls the need to manage every water drop to attain food security and food safety in Africa. This raises awareness that water for agricultural production is a pressing issue.

It has been noted that agricultural developments require a consistent and sustainable provision of large quantities of good quality water for food security [35]. The present situation is a clear sign that previous potential solutions to solving Africa's food insecurity have not received the most needed attention when defining development goals on the continent. Societies depend on water availability to meet a wide range of needs including water for irrigation, domestic, and industrial use.

Poverty and water are inextricably intertwined. Food security cannot be achieved without tackling water issues since lack of safe water underpins food insecurity. Countries continue to invest in the protection and management of water resources to continue deriving benefits for improved living standards. Undoubtedly, major water investments in agriculture are necessary toward meeting food production needs [35]. Crucial role players are needed to put together efforts to conserve water for a food secure world.

4.1 Water scarcity impacts on food security

Many Africans depend on aquatic and riparian plants and animals as an important source of food for both humans and livestock. These include fish, shellfish, bait, edible plants, and grazing. In addition, some areas such as wetlands and floodplains across Africa may be used for the cultivation of food crops. In this way, these riparian areas contribute to food security and livelihoods. These services are of particular importance to poor communities [36].

Nonetheless, the provision of reliable sources of water whether for small-scale water for food processing or large-scale water for irrigation is necessary to move beyond subsistence farming toward a more food secure continent [37]. The availability of water allows farmers to continue growing crops of high value such as vegetables, which are highly sensitive to water stress periods [38].

Although quality of water is crucial for peoples' nutrition and water availability for food security in developing countries [39], water investments have been rapidly declining. While irrigation has a high potential for environmental damages or disturbances, it has contributed positively to poverty eradication [39]. Irrigated agriculture has benefited both rural and urban poor by lowering food prices [39]. The availability of water for irrigation means less people fall below the poverty line, and that poor communities, women in particular, also benefit greatly from irrigation as a major source of water for most of their domestic uses, fishing, small and/or informal businesses [39].

Nonetheless, small-scale water availability can impact on food security positively. The availability of water for small-scale harvesting has a huge effect on incomes and food security in developing and poorest communities. Major water investments will have more drastic and positive impacts on the poorest communities, where the majority of people live on less than US$1 on a daily basis [39].

Existing challenges between water availability, quality, and sustainable agriculture linkages must be explored and be made explicit in planning potential agriculture-based strategies for improving food security. The need for fresh clean water is, however, threatened by the changing quantity and quality of the freshwater resources on which people depend for survival. The need for clean water is also linked to adequate sanitation and improved health [14]. Proper sanitation helps to protect water sources from bacterial, viral, and protozoal agents that cause water-related diseases. The concern for many is how can water quality be attained?

5. Water quality management

As much as water is an essential component of life, it is a hotbed for carriers of many diseases caused by consuming unclean water. Access to safe drinking-water, sanitation, and hygiene (WASH) services is an important element of food security and has a positive impact on nutrition [40]. A number of approaches are used to assess water pollution effects on the ecosystems which have a direct contribution to food security and nutrition.

A common approach is to use chemical indicators to measure the concentration of chemicals or toxicants within a water body using either water samples or direct in-stream measurement of the water source using water samples as (chemical indicators). If the chemicals within the water are in exceedance with acceptable limits, that water system is regarded as polluted and not fit for human consumption. Biomonitoring can also be used to assess water quality by examining the presence or absence of certain species or organisms in a water body [41].

Another approach that is used to assess water pollution is ecotoxicology. An investigation is conducted to examine responses of insects, fish, and other invertebrates to a chemical or stressor as biological indicators of water quality [42]. Thus, polluted aquatic systems may not adequately support the provision of fish and insects as food for humans. Similarly, necessary microbes that support plant growth in soils may not thrive in polluted environments, thereby affecting food security.

Without good quality water, the lives of millions of people especially young children are at risk of dying from preventable diseases caused by poor water, and a lack of sanitation and hygiene. There is a growing interest to better understand and measure the effect of programs and approaches not only directed toward improving water management in agriculture and food production but also to include integrated approach to implementing safe water and adequate sanitation [40]. Approaches and practices for ongoing efforts to better link WASH and nutrition programs integrating WASH into food security and nutrition programs are discussed in the following section.

5.1 Water, sanitation, and hygiene (WASH) programs and food security

The World Health Organization [43] report defines drinking water as water with acceptable quality in terms of its chemical, bacteriological, and physical parameters for safe human consumption. Estimates indicate that about 80% of all sicknesses and diseases on a global scale are linked to consumption of unclean and unsafe water and poor sanitation.

However, the quality of any water is influenced by both natural and human factors [44]. Without human influences, water quality would be determined by natural factors and/or processes such as bedrock minerals, deposition of dust, natural leaching of soil minerals and organic matter, and biological processes, among others. Water quality is determined by using water quality guidelines or standards to make a comparison between the physical and chemical characteristics of water samples. The guidelines and standards are developed to ensure the safe consumption of water and protection of ecosystems.

Africa with its soaring human population continues to experience a decline in water quality [43, 44]. Adequate water, sanitation, and hygiene are essential components for reducing poverty, illness, and death and bring about an improved socio-economic development. Poor WASH programs expose people to water-borne diseases, resulting in death and disabilities in certain cases [44]. The United Nations International Children's Emergency Fund (UNICEF) report revealed that the absence of toilets results in the contamination of water resources, while a lack of clean water impedes on basic hygiene [45]. However, increasing WASH programs have led to increased access to adequate drinking water sources and improved sanitation globally since 1990 [43].

To explore how WASH programs could improve the water and sanitation conditions for poor and developing countries across Africa, it is important to define hygiene and sanitation. Peal et al. [46] defined "sanitation" as the treatment and management of human excreta from coming into contact with humans, while "hygiene" is a required action to avoid the transmission of diseases within and between different communities. WASH programs are vital for helping people avoid contaminating water sources, which in turn improves their access and the overall food safety and security.

WASH programs also help to improve water quality for adequate food production due to their design nature, whereby communities work together to disseminate WASH information for a more collaborative program and implementation [46]. Here, practitioners work together with communities and local authorities to deliver the components of the WASH program on-site. This is complemented by practitioners revisiting the communities or distributing surveys for monitoring and evaluation purpose. Therefore, WASH program approaches have the potential to improve food security within the poor and developing African countries.

6. Effects of water pollution on food security

Water pollution is the building up of one or more substances in water to an extent that they cause water-related problems for people and animals [47]. It is a complex problem that is underpinned by many causes, which makes it difficult to solve. Increasing human population continues to exert immense pressure on the world's water resources [29]. Both urbanization and industrial revolutions have exacerbated water pollution through effluent and untreated wastewater discharges.

Irrigated agriculture has resulted in increased salinity of freshwater bodies as salts are flushed out from soils [48]. When farmers fertilize their fields or control insects using herbicides, the chemicals used get washed away as salts through surface run-off into nearby water systems. Toxic chemicals released into the atmosphere by industries can also enter into water systems as acid rain [49].

An increase in water salinity negatively impacts on the survival of aquatic macroinvertebrates, while some crops become intolerant to high soil salinities if thresholds are exceeded [50]. As a consequence, soil productivity is affected and can lead to low crop production and food insecurity. It is therefore clear that low crop production is not only an issue in semi-arid regions but also areas that receive plenteous rainfall.

Thompson and Darwish [49] argued that the poor quality of water has a direct impact on food security, with metals detected in some edible food in China, posing a high health-related risk to consumers. If pollution effects are properly monitored using the approaches outlined above, Africa can produce quality food for its citizens. However, the UNICEF [45] report outlines the importance of educating people on water quality issues as another approach to solving water pollution.

Further, strict environmental laws are necessary to minimize water pollution. For example, environmental reports indicate that the "polluter pays" principle is effective in tackling pollution [49]. The polluter principle makes it less expensive for humans to behave in an environmental cautious and/or responsible manner. It is sad, to note, however, that some countries considered to have the best water laws in Africa and beyond, such as South Africa [51], are still struggling to deal with historical water quality issues that subsequently impact on their food security. Further, unstable countries due to political reasons such as Libya would greatly be affected by food insecurities considering their dry nature. The water quality of both countries is discussed in the following sections.

6.1 South Africa: a country with poor water quality

South Africa has sufficient water to meet all the needs of the country until the year 2025 and beyond [37]. However, the country is faced with challenges related to water quality, which impedes on food production to meet people's demand for food. Poor water quality renders water unusable. Changes in agricultural practices and the expansion of urban settlements have a serious effect on the quality of water [37]. Furthermore, acid mine drainage (AMD), pesticides from agricultural practices, unmonitored sewerage systems, domestic water usage like washing clothes on the river and dumping waste in water sources in some areas of the country, and salinization from the weathering of minerals all pollute water [42, 52, 53]. Once water is polluted, it may be difficult and extremely expensive to redress, particularly in the case of underground water, which may affect agricultural production in terms of excessive salts on the soil and usable water for food production. It is thus important to note that good water quality would be suitable for food production to ensure food security.

6.2 Libya: a country in a political crisis

Libya has a rapid growing demand for freshwater availability while the water supply is limited [54]. The issue of severe water deficits as a result of nonending water demands in Libya has become more problematic for the increasing population under low rainfall, which is a result of climate change. Furthermore, the country has been experiencing high rates of pollution and depletion due to water resource unavailability. This has had major impacts on Libya's economy and social and environmental resistance capacity.

Considering that Libya is one of the driest countries on a global scale with high temperatures, meeting and maintaining acceptable living standards for the future is extremely difficult, especially in relation to food security. Food sufficiency remains uncertain in Libya due to its political instability coupled with poor water quality and soaring human population [54]. The country is likely to experience severe and most devastating situations and high risks of food insecurity and malnutrition with current political instabilities.

7. Water and food safety

This section discusses the relationship between water and food safety. Water is seen as an essential component in the food chain, starting from production, processing, and eventually consumption. In addition, water pollution has historically impacted on food safety, which constitutes an important threat to human health, food, and nutritional security. In most sub-Sahara African countries, food safety problems vary in nature, severity, and extent. These challenges are often exacerbated by the effect of climate change and natural disasters such as floods and hurricanes, whereby food may become contaminated by surface water that has itself been contaminated by sewage and wastewaters. It is well documented that flood waters often pick up large quantities of wastes and pathogenic bacteria from farms, sewer systems, latrines, and septic tanks. Overcrowding of the survivors after disasters may aggravate the situation, particularly if sanitary conditions are poor.

Any breakdown in vital services, such as water supply or electricity, also adversely affects the quality of food. In the absence of electricity, cold storage may be more difficult, if not impossible, and foods may be subject to bacterial growth. This may be obtained at any stage of the food chain, from production to consumption. Lack of safe drinking water and sanitation hampers the hygienic preparation of food and increases the risk of food contamination.

Food safety has become a constant global concern apart from affecting human health; factors such as international trade and food security are also influenced. Consequently, most research institutions, healthcare institutions, and governments of several African countries have conducted comprehensive studies on the effect of water on food safety in various production chains. According to a recent study, the main water issues that affect food safety in low income countries include bacterial pathogens, followed by pesticide residues and healthy diet [40]. Although the reported evidence of food-borne disease is still limited, the known incidences of food borne disease in low income countries such as sub-Saharan African largely emanate from three major sources, namely biological hazards and chemical and physical contamination.

7.1 Biological water contaminants

Water and food contaminated by microorganisms are major contributing factors for the emerging diarrheal diseases in the developing countries, and over 1 billion children under the age of 5 years are affected worldwide [26]. The high prevalence of deaths related to food and water contamination in developing countries could be attributed to several factors. For example, in many African countries, milk and dairy production constitute an important source of livelihoods for most peasant and smallholder farmers. Furthermore, animal production has become part of agricultural diversification strategy for most African countries in an attempt to ensure food security. The intensification of animal production has also generated a considerable impact on the environment considering the fact that milk provides suitable condition for the growth of different kinds of microorganisms, and microbial hazards are the most important concern within the dairy industry.

Biological agents associated with water contamination that have an impact on food safety include enteric pathogens such as bacteria, viruses, and protozoa. A study conducted in North-West Province of South Africa reported that multi-drug resistant *Staphylococcus aureus* strains were detected in samples of raw, bulk, and pasteurized milk [43]. Other common biological contaminants are *Escherichia coli*. The *E. coli* bacteria belong to the intestinal microbiota of humans and animals and are generally not harmful. Certain *E. coli* strains, however, harbor virulence factors and can cause intestinal and extra-intestinal diseases. For example, Shiga toxin-producing *Escherichia coli* zoonotic bacteria have globally been associated with various foods of animal origin, especially beef and sheep meat [40].

Apart from animal product contamination, biological contaminants may also occur in crop products. Foodborne outbreaks from fruit and vegetable produce have caused economic loss, food wastage and loss confidence regarding the safety of fresh produce from most African countries. Studies on the safety of fresh produce have identified water as one of the key risk factors that contribute to contamination of the farm produce. Indeed, studies have shown that most foodborne diseases are caused by consumption of fresh, perishable foods sold in informal markets [44].

7.2 Chemical hazards

Generally, mycotoxins, heavy metals, and over-application of fertilizers and pesticides are considered to be the most important chemical factors impacting on food safety in most developing countries including the African region [45]. In nature, thousands of mycotoxins occur but only a few of them present significant food safety challenges.

Mycotoxins are secondary metabolites mainly produced by fungal species from the *Aspergillus, Penicillium, and Fusarium genera*. They often develop during production, harvest, and storage of grains and nuts in the presence of water [45]. In the food production process, mycotoxins are among the most potent mutagenic and carcinogenic substances known. Ingestion of mycotoxins poses chronic health risks such as hepatotoxicity, genotoxicity, suppression of immunity, estrogenicity, nephrotoxicity, teratogenicity, and carcinogenic effects [44].

The adverse health effects of mycotoxins are compounded by the fact that they are not completely eliminated during food processing operations and can contaminate finished processed food products [55]. The presence of mycotoxins, particularly the aflatoxins, has generated a lot of interest in the food products from African countries. The work by Maxwell (1998) evaluated the presence of aflatoxins in human body fluids and tissues in relation to child health in the tropics. The findings showed that in Ghana, Kenya, Nigeria, and Sierra Leone, 25% of cord blood samples contained aflatoxins, ranging from 7 ng/L to 65 μg/L. The major classes of aflatoxins that were identified in the African countries include B1 and M1. **Figure 1** shows the chemical structures of the most prevalent aflatoxins in African countries.

Heavy metals have also contributed negatively to the food safety status in most African countries. As such, human exposure to heavy metals in Africa has become

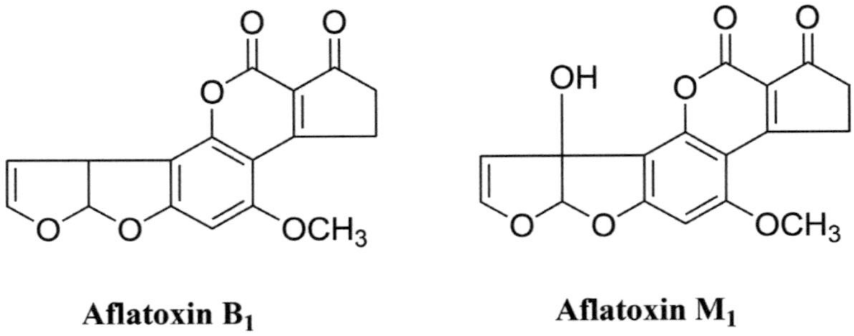

Figure 1.
Chemical structures of aflatoxins prevalent in African countries.

a major health risk and has received the attention of national and international environmentalists [47]. Rapid population growth, increasing urbanization, and the increasing appearance of slums and townships as a consequence of poor planning coupled with increasing industrial activities are some of the major factors that have contributed to the accumulation of heavy metals in food products. Africa has large deposits of mineral resources, and mining activities have increased with poor environmental regulations and compliance. Thus, heavy metals have constituted agents of toxic pollution of water, air, soil, and food products.

An environmental assessment report by the United Nations Environment Programme (UNEP) released in 2011, showed that drinking water, air, and agricultural soil in 10 communities from southeastern Nigeria contained over 900 times permissible levels of hydrocarbon and heavy metals [47]. The report further indicated that heavy metal pollution is a continental public health challenge in the sub-Saharan African region. Another study conducted in the Democratic Republic of Congo showed a 43-fold increase in the urinary concentration of cadmium, cobalt, lead, and uranium in human subjects including children living in mining areas compared to controls [56]. The increase in the levels of the heavy metals was largely attributed to ingestion of contaminated food products and water with toxic chemical compounds. The increasing negative effects on food safety from water and soil pollution have, therefore, potentially put more people at risk of carcinogenic diseases, particularly in food producing areas.

8. Conclusion

Water is the most vital natural resource on the planet that many life forms depend on for survival. This chapter has shown how population growth, competition for water across sectors, and the exposure to infectious agents or toxic chemicals pose a serious threat to water security, food security, and human existence. There is increased pressure on all sectors to minimize water use by considering more efficient use of water and alternative sources of water. This is only possible if the normative criteria of the human right to safe drinking water which are accessibility, availability, and quality are enforced to ensure that all current and foreseeable water demands highlighted under SDG 6 are met. Little promising progress has been achieved, but much work still has to be done to make water sustainability a reality before the SDG target date of 2030. The present status of water potential in Africa suggests that synergies that adopt sharing of expertise, experiences, knowledge, analytical capabilities, and optimizing mechanisms for greater food safety assurance and awareness by looking at both chemical and microbial hazards in foods should be promoted in the continent.

DOI: http://dx.doi.org/10.5772/intechopen.86788

Author details

Nokuthula Vilakazi[1*], Kumbukani Nyirenda[1,2] and Emmanuel Vellemu[1,3]

1 Future Africa, University of Pretoria, South Africa

2 College of Medicine, University of Malawi, Blantyre, Malawi

3 Department of Water Resources Management, Malawi University of Science and Technology, Limbe, Malawi

*Address all correspondence to: nokuthula.vilakazi@fabi.up.ac.za

References

[1] Global Water Partnership (GWP). Global Water Partnership Strategy 2009-2013. Stockholm, Sweden; 2009

[2] UN Water. Integrated Monitoring Guide for SDG 6: Targets and Global Indicators. 2017. pp. 1-26

[3] United Nations. Consultation Background Document 1 Global Health and Foreign Policy: Strategic Opportunities and Challenges; 2009

[4] Millennium Ecosystems Assessment (MEA). Ecosystems and Human Well-Being: Current State and Trends: Dryland Systems; 2005

[5] Millennium Ecosystem Assessment (MEA). Fresh Water; Washington, DC; 2005

[6] Douglas I. Reference Module in Earth Systems and Environmental Sciences; Elsevier; 2015

[7] NHMRC. Water, Australia; 2006

[8] Zimmerman M, Snow B. An Introduction to Nutrition. Vol. 1.0; 2012

[9] Jéquier E, Constant F. Water as an essential nutrient: The physiological basis of hydration. European Journal of Clinical Nutrition. 2010;**64**(2):115-123

[10] Kleiner SM. Water. Journal of the American Dietetic Association. 1999;**99**(2):200-206

[11] Lang F, Waldegger S. Regulating Cell Volume [Online]. 1997. Available from: https://studylib.net/doc/7645794/regulating-cell-volume [Accessed: May 5, 2019]

[12] Mudambi S. Fundamentals of Foods, Nutrition and Diet Therapy. 5th ed. New Age International Pty Ltd Publishers; 2007. p. 128-135

[13] McNeil VH, Cox ME. Defining the climatic signal in stream salinity trends using the Interdecadal Pacific Oscillation and its rate of change. Hydrology and Earth System Sciences. 2007;**11**(4):1295-1307

[14] Gleick PH. Basic water requirements for human activities: Meeting basic needs. Water International. 1996;**21**(2):83-92

[15] Portis AJ, Sundaram CP. Diagnosis and initial management of kidney stones. American Family Physician. 2001;**63**(7):1329-1338

[16] Howard G, Bartram J. Sanitation and Health Programme; 2003

[17] Suting BM. Assessing the knowledge regarding environmental sanitation and its impact on health among the people in a selected rural community of Meghalaya. The Nursing Journal of India. 2016;**107**(4):153-155

[18] Muller M, Schreiner B, Smith L, Van Koppen B, Sally H, Aliber M, et al. Water Security in South Africa. Development Planning Division. Working Paper Series. No. 12; 2009

[19] UNICEF. Progress on Drinking Water, Sanitation and Hygiene Update and SDG Baselines 2017 Launch version July 12 Main Report; 2017

[20] Mekonnen MM, Hoekstra AY. Four billion people facing severe water scarcity. Science Advances. 2016;**2**(2):e1500323

[21] OECD. Agriculture Policy Notes; OECD [Online]. Available from: http://www.oecd.org/tad/agriculture-policy-notes.htm [Accessed: May 5, 2019]

[22] Gleick PH. The World's Water. Volume 8: The Biennial Report On Freshwater Resources. 2014;**8**

[23] Shiklomanov IA. World Water Resources a New Appraisal and Assessment for the 21st Century a Summary of the Monograph World Water Resources Prepared in the Framework of The International Hydrological Programme. 1991;**25**

[24] Cosgrove WJ, Loucks DP. Water management: Current and future challenges and research directions. Water Resources Research. 2015;**51**:4823-4839

[25] Strzepek K, Boehlert B. Competition for water for the food system. Philosophical Transactions of the Royal Society B. 2010;**365**(1554):2927-2940

[26] Ritchie H, Roser M. Water Use and Sanitation, Our World Data; 2017

[27] Grey D, Sadoff CW. Sink or Swim? Water Security for Growth and Development

[28] Lal R. World water resources and achieving water security. Agronomy Journal. 2015;**107**(4):1526

[29] Mabhaudhi T, Chibarabada T, Modi A, Mabhaudhi T, Chibarabada T, Modi A. Water-food-nutrition-health nexus: Linking water to improving food, nutrition and health in Sub-Saharan Africa. International Journal of Environmental Research and Public Health. 2016;**13**(1):107

[30] Senker P. Foresight: The future of food and farming, final project report. Prometheus. 2011;**29**(3):309-313

[31] Davies WJ, Zhang J, Yang J, Dodd IC. Novel crop science to improve yield and resource use efficiency in water-limited agriculture. The Journal of Agricultural Science. 2011;**149**(S1):123-131

[32] Earle A. The Role of Virtual Water in Food Security in Southern Africa; 2001

[33] H. Level Panel of Experts on Food Security. The High Level Panel of Experts on Food Security and Nutrition Nutrition and Food Systems; 2017

[34] Newborne P, Mason N. The private Sector's contribution to water management: Re-examining corporate Purposes and company roles. Water Alternatives. 2012;**5**(30):603-618

[35] Elhassadi A. Pollution of water resources from industrial effluents: a case study—Benghazi, Libya. Desalination. 2008;**222**(1-3):286-293

[36] Department of Water Affairs (DWA). Resource Directed Management of Water Quality: Planning Level Review of Water Quality in South Africa, Sub-seriesWQP No. 2.0; Pretoria, South Africa; 2011

[37] McLachlan M, Thorne J, Battersby-Lennard J, Drimie S, Fincham R, Frayne B, et al. Seeding change: A proposal for renewal in the South African food system. Development Planning Division. Working Paper Series No. 16. 2009

[38] Molden DJ, Fraiture C. Investing in Water for Food, Ecosystems and Livelihoods. Sri Lanka; 2004

[39] Rijsberman FR. Water scarcity: Fact or fiction? Agricultural Water Management. 2006;**80**(1-3):5-22

[40] Uyttendaele M, Franz E, Schlüter O. Food safety, a global challenge. International Journal of Environmental Research and Public Health. 2015;**13**(1):1-6

[41] Odume ON. An Evaluation of Macroinvertebrate-Based Biomonitoring and Ecotoxicological Assessments of Deteriorating Environmental Water Quality in the Swartkops River, South Africa. Rhodes University; 2014

[42] Mensah PK. Environmental Water Quality Management of Glyphosate-Based Herbicides in South Africa. Rhodes University; 2012

[43] Akindolire M, Babalola O, Ateba C. Detection of antibiotic resistant *Staphylococcus aureus* from milk: A public health implication. International Journal of Environmental Research and Public Health. 2015;**12**(9):10254-10275

[44] Marin S, Ramos AJ, Cano-Sancho G, Sanchis V. Mycotoxins: Occurrence, toxicology, and exposure assessment. Food and Chemical Toxicology. 2013;**60**:218-237

[45] Smith M-C, Madec S, Coton E, Hymery N. Natural co-occurrence of mycotoxins in foods and feeds and their in vitro combined toxicological effects. Toxins. 2016;**8**(4):94

[46] Peal A, Evans B, van der Voorden C. Hygiene and Sanitation Software: An Overview of Approaches. Geneva; 2010

[47] United Nations Environment Programme (UNEP). Global Drylands: A UN System-Wide Response; 2011

[48] Eerkes-Medrano D, Thompson RC, Aldridge DC. Microplastics in freshwater systems: A review of the emerging threats, identification of knowledge gaps and prioritisation of research needs. Water Research. 2015;**75**:63-82

[49] Thompson LA, Darwish WS. Environmental chemical contaminants in food: Review of a global problem. Journal of Toxicology. 2019;**2019**:1-14

[50] Vellemu EC, Mensah PK, Griffin N, Odume ON. Derivation of scenario-specific water quality guidelines for acid mine drainage in South Africa, using a risk-based approach. African Journal of Aquatic Science. 2018;**43**(1):51-58

[51] Griffin NJ, Palmer CG. Draft Report on the Status and Trends of Selected Water Quality Parameters in the Olifants River. Grahamstown; 2015

[52] McCarthy TS. The impact of acid mine drainage in South Africa. South African Journal of Science. 2011;**107**(5-6):01-07

[53] Vellemu EC, Mensah PK, Griffin NJ, Odume ON. Sensitivity of the mayfly Adenophlebia auriculata (Ephemeroptera: Leptophlebiidae) to $MgSO_4$ and Na_2SO_4. Physics and Chemistry of the Earth, Parts A/B/C. 2017;**100**:81-85

[54] Wheida E, Verhoeven R. An alternative solution of the water shortage problem in Libya. Water Resources Management. 2007;**21**(6):961-982

[55] Bullerman LB, Bianchini A. Stability of mycotoxins during food processing. International Journal of Food Microbiology. 2007;**119**(1-2):140-146

[56] Fasinu P, Orisakwe OE. Heavy metal pollution in sub-Saharan Africa and possible implications in cancer epidemiology. Asian Pacific Journal of Cancer Prevention. 2013;**14**(6):3393-3402

Chapter 4

Food Safety and Food Security in the Informal Sector

Bukelwa Grwambi

Abstract

Food markets in the informal sector play a vital role in the livelihoods of the poor in developing countries. However, the conditions under which the informal sector operates raise concerns relating to the safety and quality of food sold. This chapter makes reference to case studies conducted by the International Livestock Research Institute's Safe Food Fair Food project to facilitate the implementation of food safety in Sub-Saharan Africa. The purpose is to illustrate the relevance and applicability of a food chain approach in the implementation of food safety in the informal sector. Results show that some milk gets contaminated during milking, processing, cooling and handling. Such practices as adulteration and pooling were also reported to contaminate milk. The chapter concludes that it is the responsibility of all stakeholders to ensure the safety of milk along the chain.

Keywords: foodborne illnesses, food chain, milk, contamination

1. Introduction

Informal economies have long been the linchpin of food security for both the rural and urban poor in developing countries [1]. The most visible activities in the informal sector are food production (urban, peri-urban and rural), processing, catering and transport and retail sale of fresh or prepared products (e.g. street food) with women being responsible for small catering operations and street food sales [2]. Women are traditionally skilled in these activities and already have the necessary cooking utensils at home, while the food they prepare also enables them to feed their families [3].

Most of the eggs, fish, meat and milk sold to the poor in urban Africa are sourced from informal markets [4]. For example, in countries like Kenya, Mali and Uganda, 80–90% of raw milk is purchased from vendors or small-scale retailers in informal markets [4]. Informal markets in this regard contribute to food security and do so in various ways. First, informal markets tend to be located closer to low-income housing settlements and thus serve as the main source of food for many of the urban poor [1]. Second, informal vendors can sell in smaller quantities, at lower prices and on credit, thus making food affordable to marginalised consumers [2, 5]. Third, the many points of sale near schools and offices, bus stops and stations facilitate access to food, thus saving consumers' time and transport costs [2]. Fourth, the ability of poorer households to produce their own food products especially in situations of economic uncertainty can be crucial for food security [2].

Despite this contribution to food security, the safety of food sold in the informal sector has been raised as a matter of concern. Traders in informal markets operate in settings without electricity, clean potable water, waste disposal and sanitation facilities [4, 5]. These settings are sometimes dusty and muddy and/or may sometimes be flooded due to poor roads [6]. Such an environment exposes food to contamination, thus increasing the risk of foodborne illnesses [6].

The implementation of food safety in the informal sector has traditionally focused on enforcement mechanisms to remove "unsafe" food from the market [3, 7]. This reactive approach which is also a response to other non-compliances of the sector such as tax evasion, trespassing on private land and traffic congestion mainly targets street vendors and typically involves issuing of fines, making of arrests, confiscation of merchandise and demolishing of market stalls [7].

The sole focus of these campaigns on street vendors in the drive towards implementation of food safety in the informal sector somehow fails to hold producers (including urban and peri-urban agriculturalists), transporters, processors (including home-based caterers), managers, small restaurant owners, members of cooperatives etc. accountable as these stakeholders also have a role to play in ensuring the production, processing, packaging and distribution of safe food along the food chain. As a result, such campaigns have been rendered ineffective (see, e.g. [1, 4]).

This chapter makes reference to case studies conducted by the International Livestock Research Institute's Safe Food Fair Food project to facilitate the implementation of food safety in Sub-Saharan Africa. The purpose is to illustrate the relevance and the applicability of a food chain approach in the implementation of food safety in the informal sector. The chapter is organised as follows. Section 2 presents a theoretical framework with the first sub-section outlining the food chain approach in the implementation of food safety followed by foodborne illnesses and their impact on public health. The methodology section follows after which we present the results. The chapter then draws conclusions and outlines implications for stakeholders concerned and some recommendations for further research.

2. Theoretical framework

2.1 The food chain approach in the implementation of food safety

For food to be regarded as safe, there should be assurance that it will not cause harm to the consumer when prepared and/or eaten according to its intended use [8].

The food chain approach acknowledges that the responsibility to provide safe, healthy and nutritious food lies with all the actors taking part in the production, processing, trade and consumption of food along the entire food chain from primary production to final consumption [3]. Chain actors include food producers, fishermen, abattoir operators, food processors and distributors including wholesalers and retailers. This responsibility extends to the end-consumer who must be educated to ensure that food is properly stored and hygienically prepared and food shelf lives are respected [3]. Government departments with a mandate to render public health services are also implicated in this regard [3].

The food chain approach uses a scientific, rational and systematic approach known as the Hazard Analysis and Critical Control Points (HACCP) to identify, assess and control hazards during production, processing, manufacturing and preparation of food. For HACCP to be effective, a strong foundation of safety-related prerequisites is essential.

Prerequisite programmes include, among others, the implementation of good manufacturing practices, good agricultural practices, good hygiene practices, sanitation, standard operating procedures, employee hygiene and training, product labelling and coding, facilities design, equipment calibration and maintenance. Food safety along the value chain thus promotes the adoption of conditions and practices that preserve the quality of food in order to prevent contamination and the resulting foodborne illnesses [8].

2.2 Food contamination and foodborne illnesses

Foodborne illnesses are diseases caused by microbiological, chemical and physical agents that enter the body through the ingestion of contaminated food and/or water used for its production, processing and preparation [2, 3, 9]. In humans, foodborne illnesses are linked to more than 250 different types of viruses, bacteria, parasites, toxins, metals and prions [10] and are usually either infectious or toxic in nature. They are at best unpleasant and at worst fatal.

The infections range from mild gastro-enteritis to life-threatening neurological, hepatic and renal syndromes caused by either toxin from the disease-causing microbes or by the human body's reaction to the microbe itself [11]. Although viruses are more responsible for more than 50% of all foodborne illnesses, generally hospitalizations and deaths associated with foodborne infections are due to bacterial agents [11]. Of the many thousands different bacterial species, more than 90% of food poisoning illnesses are caused by species of *Staphylococcus*, *Salmonella*, *Clostridium*, *Campylobacter*, *Listeria*, *Vibrio*, *Bacillus* and *Enteropathogenic coli* [12]. Around 2 million people die every year from diarrhoeal diseases largely due to contaminated food and water [2, 3].

The contamination of food may occur at any stage in the process from production to consumption (farm to fork or stable to table) and can also result from environmental contamination including pollution of water, soil or feeds [2, 3]. Improving the safety and quality of food at all stages of the food chain is therefore important in reducing the risks associated with the consumption of contaminated food and the resulting foodborne illnesses.

3. Methodology

3.1 Choice of the study area

For over a decade, the International Livestock Research Centre (ILRI) and partners have been conducting research on food safety in informal markets in Sub-Saharan Africa. The objective is to support intensification of livestock production by building capacity for better management of safety of animal source food products. The ultimate goal is to maximise market access for the poor dependent on livestock and livestock products while minimising foodborne illnesses for poor consumers [13]. While the focus of ILRI's Safe Food Fair Food project was livestock and livestock products, the majority of the cases studied milk in informal markets. This chapter therefore focuses on informal milk marketing in Sub-Saharan Africa.

3.2 Context of the study

Milk produced in the informal sector often leaves the farm gate through three channels, namely, collectors who sell the milk to the informal market, sale to the dairy cooperative and/or sale within the community [14]. Collection of milk is carried out at milk collection centres by dairy cooperatives or private milk collectors [14, 15]. Milk producers and other traders transport their milk on foot, by horse and by donkey and/or make use of a private milk transporter to deliver the milk to the milk collection centres and to the processing plant [14].

Alternatively, milk producers take their raw milk to the milk collection points. From the milk collection points, the milk is transported to a dairy plant or to the milk collection centres where it is bulked, cooled and transported to the dairy plant. Private milk collectors and dairy cooperatives operate milk collection points and milk collection centres [14]. The dairy cooperatives are mainly involved in bulk collecting of raw milk from the members in order to process the collected milk into different dairy products [14]. Informal milk marketing thus involves direct supply of fresh raw milk by small-holder dairy producers to the neighbouring final consumers and to the traders or individuals in the nearby cities.

3.3 Data collection

This chapter makes reference to case studies conducted by the International Livestock Research Institute under the Safe Food Fair Food project in Sub-Saharan Africa. Secondary data sources of information are also consulted to complement the data.

3.4 Data analysis

This chapter applies guidelines on good agricultural practices, good manufacturing practices and good hygiene practices to offer justification as to why it is important to adopt a food chain approach in the implementation of food safety initiatives in the informal sector. The chapter does so by making reference to the case studies on milk production in Sub-Saharan Africa by the International Livestock Research Institute under the Safe Food Fair Food project.

4. Food safety along the milk value chain in the informal sector

Like any other food business, milk producers must aim to ensure that the safety and quality of the raw milk produced will satisfy the highest expectations of the food industry and consumers [16].

4.1 Good agricultural practices

Good farming practices underpin the marketing of safe, quality-assured milk-based products [16]. This means that on-farm practices should ensure that milk is produced by healthy animals under acceptable conditions for the animals [16]. The focus of on-farm practices should be on preventing a problem (including animal diseases) rather than solving it after it has occurred [16]. However, according to Desissa et al. [17], 92% of dairy farmers indicated that their cows had recently experienced inflammation of the udder. Kilango et al. [18] also reported that almost 90% of the farmers had encountered udder infections in their animals. Only 21% of the farmers were reported to have used post-milking teat disinfectant which is known to be effective in preventing udder inflammation [18].

Milk producers are required to manage the use of all chemicals, e.g. detergents, disinfectants, antiparasitics, antibiotics, herbicides, pesticides and fungicides, to prevent unacceptable chemical residues occurring in the milk and unsuitable chemicals adversely affecting animal health and productivity and are expected to be aware of all chemicals that may leave residues in milk [16]. Milk producers are also required to observe withholding periods, i.e. the minimum times when milk should not be sold for human consumption after application of chemicals [16]. Interestingly, most of the farmers knew about the proper use of antibiotics to treat dairy cows and the importance of adhering to the withdrawal period for milk from cows undergoing treatment [18]. Yet in a study done by Kouame-Sina et al. [19], almost a quarter (24.7%) of the milk samples contained antibiotics.

Milking is the most important single activity in a dairy farm [16]. FAO [16] recommends that before a cow is milked, the foremilk should be extracted and checked for abnormalities. It is also expected of farmers to follow appropriate procedures to separate milk from sick animals and animals under treatment. For example, sick animals could be milked last into a separate container and/or separate facilities may be provided if possible [16]. However, Kouame-Sina et al. [19] reported that milk from cows with udder inflammation (mastitis) was still sold.

Yobouet et al. [20] and Kone et al. [21] also observed that while milking, milkers often dipped their fingers into the milk to use it as a lubricant to help them milk faster. The farmers considered it necessary to grease the teats with milk. However, this practice presented a risk of milk contamination [21].

FAO [16] recommends that the disposal of diseased and dead animals should be done in a way that minimizes the risk of disease spread. According to Sow et al. [22], about 12% of farmers reported their cows had aborted once, and approximately 2% reported that their cows aborted twice, while 27% reported their female goats had aborted once, 4% twice and 1% thrice. Almost 75% of these respondents reported they handled the aborted material of their goats; for instance, they would handle the foetus with bare hands and later burn it [22]. While the latter practice reduces the risk of transmission of brucellosis, touching the aborted material with bare hands makes transmission very likely [22].

4.2 Good manufacturing practices

Good milk is considered to be cow milk that is not mixed with that from other species or milk powder [21] or any additives or adulterants. However, it was found out that producers sometimes put additives in milk to increase fat content. They also add water in milk to increase volumes. This practice, which is commonly known as adulteration, is done in an attempt to get fair and remunerative prices for the milk. In the dairy industry in West and East Africa, it seemed to be common practice to add water to milk in order to sell large quantities. Yobouet et al. [20] also observed that adulteration of milk by adding water was relatively widespread among retailers, with 47.1% of them reportedly adding water to the milk before selling it.

Similarly, in a case study by Kouame-Sina et al. [19], 50% of the milk on sale was adulterated with water. Adulteration of milk is not only illegal but also presents a health risk to consumers if the added water is contaminated [20]. With adulteration, consumers get less of what they paid for [21]. This practice is also unethical. According to Desissa et al. [17], collection centres checked the milk for adulteration with water and contamination with hair, hay or faeces. Milk that does not pass the quality test is rejected and is mostly processed by the women into féné (partially fermented milk), which may present a health risk [21]. More than 25% of the vendors did not use any form of quality control checks before buying the milk [18] which meant that they could not establish whether the milk they bought was contaminated or not.

Because of its high perishability, holding milk for long periods without cooling it can lead to rapid growth and multiplication of the milk bacteria [18]. To sustain quality, milk is generally cooled after harvesting.

To cool the milk, some producers predominantly used package icing. The ice blocks are purchased from vendors who make them by filling polythene pouches with tap water and packing the pouches in a freezer [23]. While water and ice cooling methods provide fast initial cooling, they also feature the highest risk of contamination.

In the cases studied by Spengler et al. [24], none of the farmers in the study sites cooled the raw milk. The traders and retailers also reported that the milk they received from the farms was not cooled [20].

Pooling of milk was also reported to increase the risk of contamination. Yobouet et al. [20] reported that upon receipt of milk from farmers, traders and retailers bulked the milk in a single storage tank. This is risky because, if the milk from one supplier is contaminated, then there is a higher chance that the entire batch in the tank will be spoiled. According to Desissa et al. [17], only milk from cooperative members was purchased and pooled into a 50 litre container.

With regard to packaging, all of the vendors used plastic buckets for handling the milk, a practice that is not recommended as plastic containers are known to be vulnerable to bacterial contamination due to difficulty to sterilise [18]. This was also observed by [23].

4.3 Good hygiene practices

Workers can unintentionally contaminate milk, water supplies and equipment, thus transmitting diseases to other workers or consumers. Proper hand-washing, correct washing procedures including applying soap on wet hands, scrubbing of whole hand during a minimum of 20 s, rinsing with water, drying with paper towel (disposable) and turning off the knob with towel are recommended as part of enhancing food safety [8].

It was interesting to observe that at least some of the recommended hygiene practices were followed. However, some of the procedures applied were not completely correct which could further contaminate the milk. For example, milkers cleaned the udders of the cows either with dry hands or with water that was not of potable quality [24]. Yobouet et al. [20] and Kouame-Sina et al. [19] both observed that prior to milking, most milkers washed neither their hands nor the udders of the cows, while in other cases, the majority of the farmers washed their hands before milking [25]. Kabui et al. [25] also observed that the majority of those who washed their hands used water and soap [25], while in a case study by Kilango et al. [18], only 17% of milkers washed their hands with water and soap. Farmers only cleaned their hands with cold water from a contaminated water source [24].

Almost all milkers washed the cow udders before milking. However, most of the milkers did not dry their hands or the udders of the cows, thus increasing the risk of contamination from dirty water running into the milk [18].

Using one cloth for each cow to dry the udder is recommended as it prevents the transfer of bacteria and dirt from one animal to another. Kilango et al. [18] observed fewer milkers used one cloth per cow to dry the udder, and according to these authors, using a shared cloth for several cows may be worse than using no cloth at all [18].

Proper personal hygiene is also important to enhance food safety in informal milk markets. Regular bathing or showering, washing of hands and keeping nails clean and short and wearing of clean clothes and hair nets are thus recommended. According to Kilango et al. [18], only 59% of the staff working at milk kiosks wore clothes that were visibly clean.

Proper cleaning of milk utensils is also instrumental in the implementation of food safety in informal milk markets. About 82% of the staff used soap for washing utensils [18]. Those without basins but with running hot water cleaned the milk handling equipment in the same bowl used for washing hands [18]. This practice is not good as it may increase the risk of contamination.

5. Conclusions and recommendations

While vendors are at the forefront of milk sales in informal markets, the informal market environment seemed not to be the only source where food can get contaminated as is always perceived. Results show that some milk got contaminated during milking, cooling, pooling, processing, packaging, handling and cleaning of milking utensils which means that other stakeholders who handled the product were also responsible for milk contamination but were not held accountable for supplying a product that is "unsafe" as perceived by the authorities. Ensuring food safety along the chain therefore becomes the responsibility of everyone who has a role to play. The fact that a high number of incidents of foodborne illnesses is recorded in informal economies is also enough evidence to warrant the implementation of food safety practices in informal economies but a correct approach and strategies need to be adopted. Compliance of relevant actors with food safety principles should therefore be encouraged.

6. Implications for stakeholders along the milk value chain

These finding have implications for dairy farmers/milk producers, milkers, retailers/milk kiosks operators, milk cooperative members, processors, traders/vendors, households and consumers of milk. These stakeholders all need to be aware of food contamination and the risks and consequences of foodborne illnesses. The findings also imply that stakeholders need to be proactive in their drive to ensure food safety along the food chain which means that they need to adhere to good agricultural practices, good hygiene practices as well as good manufacturing practices. Training of households on basic hygiene is also crucial. This could also help minimise the incidents of foodborne illness that threaten the lives of consumers.

7. Recommendations for further research

To take the food safety agenda forward, future research should focus on developing a focused strategy for the implementation of food safety in the informal sector. This should take into consideration the context and the importance of food security in rural livelihoods.

Author details

Bukelwa Grwambi
Western Cape Department of Agriculture, Agricultural Economics Services, Marketing and Agribusiness Division, Elsenburg, South Africa

*Address all correspondence to: bukelwag@elsenburg.com

References

[1] Resnick D. Chapter 6: Governance: Informal food markets in Africa's cities. In: IFPRI book chapters: 2017 Global Food Policy Report. Washington, DC, USA: International Food Policy Research Institute; 2017. pp. 50-57

[2] FAO. The informal food sector: Municipal support policies for operators. A briefing guide for mayors, city executives and urban planners in developing countries and countries in transition. In: Food in Cities Collection 4. Italy, Rome; 2003a

[3] FAO. FAO's strategy for a food chain approach to food safety and quality: A framework document for the development of future strategic direction. In: Seventeenth Session, Item 5 of the Provincial Agenda. 31 March to 04 April 2003. Rome, Italy; 2003b

[4] Glatzel K. Why supporting Africa's informal markets could mean better nutrition for poor city dwellers. In: IFPRI Blog: Research Post. Washington, DC: International Food Policy Research Institute; 2017

[5] FAO. Promises and Challenges of the Informal Food Sector in Developing Countries. Rome, Italy: A joint publication by the Rural Infrastructure and Agro-industries division and the Nutrition and Consumer Protection division of the Agriculture and Consumer Protection Department of FAO. I collaboration with the Agricultural Economics and Engineering Department (University of Bologna, Italy) and the Department of Sociology and Anthropology (University of Ottawa, Canada); 2007

[6] Sverdlik A. Promoting food security, safe food trading and vendors' livelihoods in informal settlements: Lessons from Nairobi. In: Urban Zoo Policy Brief. London, UK: University College London; 2017

[7] Tinker I. Street foods: Testing assumptions about informal sector activity by women and men. Current Sociology. 1987;**35**(3):1-10

[8] UN. Safety and Quality of Fresh Fruit and Vegetables: A Training Manual for Trainers. New York and Geneva; 2007 UNCTAD/DITC/COM/2006/16

[9] Sheth M, Gurudasani R, Mudbibi R. Identification of hazards in street foods of Vadodara, India. Indian Journal of Nutrition and Dietetics. 2005;**42**:266-274

[10] Tambekar DH, Jaiswal VJ, Dhanorkar DV, Gulhane PB, Dudhane MN. Identification of microbiological hazards and safety of ready-to-eat food vended in streets of Amravati City, India. Journal of Applied Bioscience. 2008;**1**:195-201

[11] Schelin N, Wallin-Carlquist N, Cohn MT, Lindqvist R, Barker GC, Radstrom P. The formation of *Staphyllococcus areus enterotoxin* in food environments and advances in risk assessment. Virulence. 2011;**2**(6):580-592

[12] Schmidt RH, Renee MG, Archer DL, Keith RS. General overview of the causative agents of foodborne illnesses. In: FSH033. Food Science and Human Nutrition Department, Florida Cooperative Extension Service, IFAS, University of Florida; 2003. Available from: http://edis.ifas.ufl.edu/fs099

[13] Grace D, Roesel K, Makita K, Bonfoh B, Kang'ethe E, Kurwijila L, et al. Food Safety and Informal Markets. 2015

[14] Debele A. Analysis of milk value chain: The case of Ada'a dairy cooperative in Ada'a district, East Shawa zone of Oronia regional state, Ethiopia [Masters thesis]. Leeuwarden,

the Netherlands: Van Hall Larenstein University; 2012

[15] Salla A. Review of the Livestock and Milk Value Chains and Policy Influencing Them in West Africa. Rome, Italy: FAO and ECOWAS; 2017

[16] FAO. Guide to Good Dairy Farming Practice. Italy, Rome: International Dairy Federation and the Food and Agriculture Organization of the United Nations; 2004

[17] Desissa F, Makita K, Teklu A, Zewde G, Grace D. Quantitative risk assessment of consuming milk contaminated with *Staphylococcus aureus* in Debre Zeit, Ethiopia. In: Roesel K, Grace D, editors. Food Safety and Informal Markets: Animal Products in Sub-Saharan Africa. New York: Routledge; 2015

[18] Kilango K, Makita K, Kurwijila L, Grace D. Food safety in milk markets of smallholder farmers in Tanzania: A case study of peri-urban wards in Temeke. In: Roesel K, Grace D, editors. Food Safety and Informal Markets: Animal Products in Sub-Saharan Africa. New York: Routledge; 2015

[19] Kouame-Sina SM, Yobouet AB, Costard S, Dadie A, Makita K, Grace D, et al. Bacterial risk assessment in informally produced milk consumed in Cote d' Ivoire. In: Roesel K, Grace D, editors. Food Safety and Informal Markets: Animal Products in Sub-Saharan Africa. New York: Routledge; 2015

[20] Yobouet AB, Kouame-Sina SM, Dadie A, Makita K, Grace D, Meile L, et al. *Bacillus cereus* risk assessment in raw milk produced in traditional dairy farms and consumed in the informal dairy sector in Abidjan, Cote d' Ivoire. In: Roesel K, Grace D, editors. Food Safety and Informal Markets: Animal Products in Sub-Saharan Africa. New York: Routledge; 2015

[21] Kone VB, Fokou G, Makita K, Grace D, Gnabeli YR, Bonfoh B. Social representation and perception of the quality of animal source food in Cinzana, Mali. In: Roesel K, Grace D, editors. Food Safety and Informal Markets: Animal Products in Sub-Saharan Africa. New York: Routledge; 2015

[22] Sow I, Makita K, Grace D, Costard S, Bonfoh B. Investigation on the risk of brucellosis linked to the production of milk in rural Cinzana, Mali. In: Roesel K, Grace D, editors. Food Safety and Informal Markets: Animal Products in Sub-Saharan Africa. New York: Routledge; 2015

[23] Appiah J, Tano-Debrah K, Amoa BB, Alpha MM, Makita K, Grace D. Assessment of the risk of consuming milk/milk products from informal markets contaminated with *Listeria monocytogenes*. In: Roesel K, Grace D, editors. Food Safety and Informal Markets: Animal Products in Sub-Saharan Africa. New York: Routledge; 2015

[24] Spengler M, Amenu K, Zarale AV, Markemann A. Assessment of water and milk quality in rural mixed crop-livestock farming systems: A case study of Lume and Siraro district, Ethiopia. In: Roesel K, Grace D, editors. Food Safety and Informal Markets: Animal Products in Sub-Saharan Africa. New York: Routledge; 2015

[25] Kabui K, Arimi SM, Kang'ethe EK, Omore A, Grace D. Milk quality control by bacteriological and compositional quality-based payment system in smallholder farms in Limuru and Eldoret, Kenya. In: Roesel K, Grace D, editors. Food Safety and Informal Markets: Animal Products in Sub-Saharan Africa. 2015

Chapter 5

The Role of Small-Scale Farmers in Ensuring Food Security in Africa

Samkelisiwe Nosipho Hlophe-Ginindza and N.S. Mpandeli

Abstract

This chapter focuses on the role of African small-scale farmers in ensuring food security going into the future and the support they will need to face the projected climatic conditions. Severe climatic conditions contribute to the uncertainty in water availability for future agricultural production. Adapting to climate change and ensuring food security requires dynamic interventions that will lead to the transformation of current farming and food production patterns as well as food distribution. Nearly 95% of Africa's agriculture is rainfed; therefore, developing and promoting rain-fed small-scale agricultural activities is a cost-effective approach for transforming rural areas in Africa and ensuring food security at local and regional levels. This is crucial in reducing vulnerability to climate change and for building sustainable livelihoods.

Keywords: Africa, small-scale famers, food security, rain-fed agriculture

1. Introduction

The world population is expected to grow by more than one-third, that is, 2.3 billion people, between the years 2009 and 2050. This growth is slower than the one seen in the past four decades, where the population grew by more than 90% (3.3 billion people). Nearly all the predicted growth is to take place in the developing world, predominantly in Africa. The fastest growth (+114%) is forecasted for sub-Saharan Africa and the slowest growth (+13%) for East and Southeast Asia [1].

Food security exists when all people in a society have adequate food for an active, healthy life at all times [2]. As a broad term, 'food security' is defined by: (1) the availability of safe and nutritious food and (2) a guaranteed capability to procure and acquire food of good quality in a socially acceptable way. Food insecurity on the other hand occurs when basic healthy food is not easily accessible, and poor households struggle to secure enough food for their nutritional needs [3]. Food insecurity has been identified as a global crisis [4].

Food insecurity is a major challenge in African countries where the rate at which the population grows far exceeds both the quantity and quality of food required to sustain the population (**Figure 1**). It is reported that 204 million of the 814 million undernourished people in the world live in sub-Saharan Africa [3]. The root causes of hunger are poverty and poor food distribution. The majority of poor households in sub-Saharan Africa are struggling to access high national and healthy food. Food insecurity and hunger in sub-Saharan Africa are caused by agricultural policy uncertain such as land reform and expropriation land without compensation. Increased food requirements from a growing world population will only escalate existing food

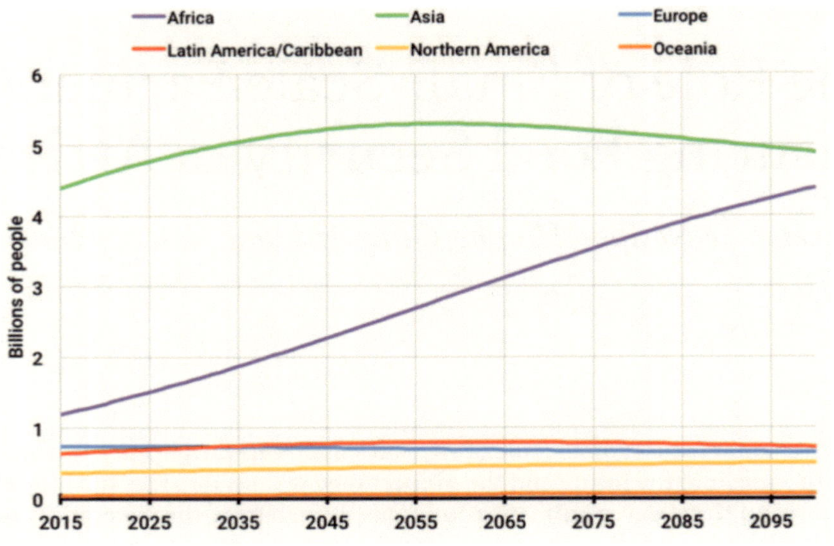

Figure 1.
Population projections. Source: [1].

security problems. The United Nations estimates that by 2050, 86% of the world's population living in extreme poverty will be concentrated in sub-Saharan Africa [1]. And in order to ensure food security in the future, current food production levels will need to be increased by at least 70% [1].

Projected climate change and unexpected extreme weather events will worsen the fragile agricultural systems, negatively affecting the natural resource base, particularly in places prone to soil degradation, water scarcity and desertification [5]. The sub-Saharan Africa is well known for relying heavy on rainfed agriculture, however, due to threats posed by extreme climatic events, high climate variability and change, the majority of the climate sensitive sectors are struggling to cope and adapt to challenges posed this natural vagaries. The general effect of climate change on agriculture will differ between different geographic regions, and it will still be difficult for farmers to plan and manage production while preventing crop losses or outbreaks of pests and diseases.

2. Food demand and production

Most of the poor population in Africa depends on agriculture, particularly small-scale farming, as the primary source of their livelihoods. Ensuring food security and poverty reduction in many African countries depends largely on the on the growth and development of the agricultural sector [6]. Agriculture in Africa is dominated by small-scale famers who rely on family labour; with 33 million farms that are less than 2 ha, small-scale farms represent 80% of all farms [7]. The role of small-scale farmers in ensuring food, nutrition security and sustainable rural development in Africa is becoming more crucial as the world faces increasing climate change challenges. Africa needs ecologically sound and climate-resilient farming systems to provide nutritionally balanced food and ensure food security for the most vulnerable.

Getting rural households to actively participate in small-scale agricultural activities for subsistence farming can play a vital role in minimizing the vulnerability to hunger in rural food-insecure households [8]. Studies done in different countries indicate that the gross domestic product (GDP) growth originating from

DOI: http://dx.doi.org/10.5772/intechopen.91694

agricultural activities is at least twice as effective in advancing the poorest half of a country's population than GDP growth generated from any other sector [9]. This benefit from the agricultural sector is to be anticipated considering that 75% of the poor in African countries live in the rural areas and derive their livelihood from agriculture as well as other agriculture-related activities. In another study, [10] also reported that people who depend on agriculture for their livelihood in African countries are typically much poorer than those working in other sectors; these people, however, represent a relatively large portion, often the majority, of the total number of the poor people in these countries.

The term smallholder or small-scale farmers refers to producers who farm in smallholdings [11]. This term includes farmers growing in home-food gardens or homestead gardens, irrigated farmers and people farming in rain-fed fields outside of the homestead [11]. Characteristics differentiating small-scale/smallholder from commercial farmers include scale and size of farm system, proportion of crops sold, household expenditure, and use of family labour, mechanization, capital intensity, financial ability and level of linkages with larger economic systems [11, 12].

According to Antonaci et al. [13], 80% of the food produced in sub-Saharan Africa is produced by smallholder farmers and these farmers are also the largest employers for the local labour force in these countries. This is partly because poverty is still a major challenge in sub-Saharan Africa and also because the agricultural sector also contributes a large share of the GDP and employment. Agriculture employs between 60 and 90% of the total labour force in sub-Saharan Africa [14].

3. Impact of climate change on the productivity of small-scale farmers

Climate change has had and will continue to have a significant impact on the livelihoods and food security of the rural poor in developing African countries. The 4th Assessment Report of the Intergovernmental Panel on Climate Change (IPCC) forecasts that climate change is expected to have a significant effect on water availability and agricultural production in many African countries. Projections by [15] suggest that when the effects of climate change are not considered, the total production of major agricultural products (cereals, fruits and vegetables oilseeds, pulses, roots and tubers, and meat) is projected to double or even triple between 2010 and 2050 (**Table 1**). However, with the inevitable adverse effect of climate change, production will be adversely affected, and different crops will be affected differently (**Table 1**). Climate change is projected to have a slightly positive effect on oilseed production and minimum effect on production of pulses, while showing and small negative

	No climate change			Effects of climate change		
	2010	2030	2050	2010	2030	2050
Cereals	114.2	178.4	237.1	108%	−2.9%	−5.1%
Fruits and vegetables	101.4	187.4	293.7	190%	−0.3%	−0.1%
Oilseeds	52.9	90	113.9	115%	0.3%	1.0%
Pulses	11.6	18.2	27.5	137%	0.0%	0.0%
Roots and tubers	224	346.6	483.2	116%	−1.0%	−1.7%
Meat	10.8	20.4	34.4	219%	−0.1%	−0.1%

Adapted from: AGRA [15].

Table 1.
Projected effect of climate change on agricultural production (million metric tons) in Africa.

effects on production of fruit and vegetables and meat [15], (**Table 1**). The projected negative effects of climate change are higher for cereals (reductions of 2.9% in 2030 and 5.1% in 2050) and roots and tubers (reductions of 1% in 2030 and 1.7% in 2050) compared to when the effect of climate change is not considered (**Table 1**).

Additionally, Makate et al. [12] found that smallholder farmers are faced with a variety of challenges, which include drought, pests and crop diseases, scarce arable land with water, lack of market availability, old age, low level of education, limited availability of quality infrastructure, lack of good cell phone network connections and limited access to quality inputs. 'A poorly functioning rural economy with undeveloped infrastructure, weak market linkages and poor agricultural support services isolates rural households from the mainstream economy and from important agricultural value-chains', reported [11].

The economies and food security of many African countries are dependent on sectors that are influenced by changing climate conditions, including agriculture, forestry, fisheries and tourism [3]. The effect of climate change is expected to vary in the different regions, for example, an increase in desertification and decrease in forest cover is expected in the arid north, with rainfall shortages predicted in the Sahara and Sahel, accompanied by soil degradation and an increasing frequency of dust storms. In West Africa, frequent and longer dry periods are projected, whereas rising sea levels will be observed in coastal areas [3].

African countries are more vulnerable to the impacts of climate change because the bulk of the population relies on rain-fed agriculture for food and their livelihoods [16]. In 2007, [17] estimated that the total agricultural yield produced in some African countries could be reduced by as much as 50% in 2020. These authors further projected that the net crop revenues could fall by 90% by the year 2100. These predictions indicate a serious threat to food security, and, by proxy, the achievement of the sustainable developmental goals set by the UN.

The deleterious effects of climate change, climate variability and food insecurity will continue to negatively impact the livelihoods of people in at-risk regions. With the increased frequency of droughts and dry spells, increasingly inconsistent rain, and heavier torrential downpours, the risk of soil erosion and vegetation damage through run-off is likely to increase. Additionally, higher than average temperatures will result in increased evapotranspiration and soil moisture evaporation rates. However, forecasts also indicate that not all changes in climate and climate variability will be negative. For instance, in some parts of the Ethiopian highlands and Mozambique, climate change effects may extend the agricultural growing season owing to increased temperatures and rainfall [14].

The inevitable change in climate necessitates regional and country initiatives to adapt. This is especially critical in African countries where vulnerability is high due to the low capacity to mitigate sudden climatic changes. Adaptation strategies are important to help farmers attain food, income as well as livelihood security despite the unpredictable climatic conditions, and extreme weather events such as droughts and floods [18, 19].

4. The potential of small-scale farmers in ensuring food security

Small-scale agriculture presents an opportunity to improve the livelihoods of the rural poor and ensure food security; however, many of the rural farmers, who had previously managed to successfully cultivate crops for subsistence use and to supplement their income, now experience poor yields or have ceased production. This can be attributed to increased urbanization, poor productivity and competition from commercial agriculture, which is producing food more effectively and at lower prices [20]. It is, therefore, imperative that small-scale farmers adopt new technologies to increase production and, consequently, ensure food security. Improved productivity of these small farmers is the key to providing practical, sustainable solutions able to address the growing problem of food security on a global scale.

Historically, a vibrant agricultural sector has, in most cases, been the foundation for positive economic growth or transformation in many developed countries. Agricultural growth was the precursor to several industrial revolutions in Europe and the United States and more recently to the industrial revolutions in China, Republic of Korea, Taiwan, Vietnam Thailand and other rapidly growing economies in Asia. At the heart of these transformations, investment in agriculture resulted in surpluses of agricultural produce; this helped to keep food prices low and played a hand in stimulating overall economic growth. This agriculture-based economic development helped to create new employment opportunities that were pivotal in absorbing the rural labour surplus. The potential of agriculture to improve a country's overall economy can never be overemphasized, [21] estimated that 1% increase in crop yields would reduce the total number of people living in poverty by 0.48% in Asia and by 0.72% in Africa.

5. Strategies to increase food production in Africa

5.1 Diversification of crops

Farming in most African countries is characterized by many small- and marginal-scale farmers with small farm holdings. These farmers produce only a limited number of crops, which occupy a relatively large portion of the production area. These 'modern' agricultural systems have degraded the natural biological interactions responsible for generating ecosystem services that are essential to agriculture, including soil fertility (nutrient cycling and retention), water-holding capacity, pest/disease control and pollination [22]. In 'modern' monocultural agricultural systems, crops rely on external nutrient inputs such as fertilizers and pesticides to replace interactions that occurred naturally. This reliance on external inputs has several consequences, including climate change, polluted air and water and the degradation of fertile soils [23]. Growing the same crops continually each year results in the emergence of several biotic and abiotic constraints and progressive reduction in yield. Therefore, crop diversification is one of the cost-effective and simple methods that can be implemented to ensure sustainable and increased agricultural production.

Increasing climate variability, fluctuating temperature and rainfall patterns, is an indicator that agricultural processes will not remain the same as crop and ecosystem responses are also expected to change. These changes comprise variations in nutrient cycling, changes in evapotranspiration, soil moisture content, as well as changes in pest incidences and plant diseases, all these entirely impact food production and food security [24, 25].

A resilient agricultural system is important in mitigating the effects of climate change. Resilience is defined as the ability or tendency of a system to maintain its organizational structure and efficiency after perturbation [26]. Therefore, a resilient agricultural system will keep producing high crop yields even after severe climate changes such as droughts or significant rainfall reductions. Crop biodiversity can therefore provide the connection between climatic stress and resilience of the system because a diversity of organisms is important for ecosystems to perform optimally and provide essential services [27].

According to Vandermeer et al. [28], crop diversification improves the functioning of an ecosystem because different species perform differing roles and consequently occupy different niches within the system. Diversification also increases ecosystem function as some components of the system may seem redundant at some point in time but become important when change in some environmental conditions is experienced. Therefore, the importance of crop diversification is that when climatic or environmental change is experienced, the redundancies within the system permit for continual functioning of the ecosystem and production of high yields [28].

Crop diversification is one of the ways small-scale farmers can use to develop a resilient agricultural system. Crop diversification forms part of the risk aversion strategy, the majority of small-scale farmers have moved away from monocropping system due to high climatic variability and change. It ensures effective use of land, water and other resources for increased yield and productivity, playing a pivotal role in poverty reduction in rural communities. Diversification in farms can also include livestock production, including aquaculture, as well as the production of commercial crops such as cotton, sugar cane, oilseeds, fruits and vegetables. Crop diversification also reduces the risk of crop failure and uncertainty due to unforeseen climate events that could adversely impact agricultural production, including the sudden onset of frost or drought and the emergence of pests [29]. This is achieved by planting crops with varying drought resistance abilities and/or selecting crops for harvest based on their seasonal suitability.

Inclusion of cash crops is particularly important for small-scale farmers in making their farms viable [30]. Diversification helps protect small-scale farmers against drops in profit that ensue if the price for a crop is lower than average in a given year [31]. This improves the purchasing power of the household, thus allowing these households to purchase other food products not produced on the farm. Consequently, farm-level crop diversification should include a wider range of crops; this way, it can contribute positively to improved health, household nutrition and food security, as well as ensuring climate resilience [32]. Thus, diversification can be used to improve and stabilize income flow, thereby providing increases in gainful employment while further reducing farm income variability.

The inclusion of horticultural crops, especially fruits and vegetables, can be used to address food and nutritional security [33]. Households practising crop diversification are more likely to have a varied diet than those who do not [32]. These authors also reported that households practising higher crop diversification are less food-insecure compared to those with relatively lower or no crop diversification.

5.2 Improve agricultural extension services

Agricultural extension can be defined as the application of scientific research and scientific principles/knowledge to agricultural practices through the education of farmers [34]. The role played by extension officers is invaluable in equipping farmers with the necessary skills to improve productivity. Agricultural extension is also critical in translating new knowledge into innovative practices [35].

The declining effectiveness of public extension services is one of the factors impeding the productivity of small-scale famers in most African countries. Increasing the productivity of small-scale farmers requires significant investment and ongoing support in agricultural extension services. Agricultural extension services can provide farmers with the vital tools and critical knowledge needed to adopt and implement new, more sustainable farming methods. Small-scale farmers face a number of risks, which require a more interactive extension system. The adoption of new technologies will serve to increase product yields, improve local food security and livelihoods, as well as build resilience against severe climate changes.

The traditional extension system, which uses a top-down approach in transferring technology, is rapidly becoming outdated in the market-oriented and more competitive climate of today's agricultural scene. In order to ensure continued and increased contribution of small-scale farmers to food security in Africa, there needs to be renewed emphasis on, as well as new approaches to, agricultural extension. The role of extension officers should not be limited to providing and transferring knowledge for increased productivity, but should also focus on new roles, including linking small-scale farmers to high value and export markets, ensuring sustainable production and mitigating the effect of climate change.

5.3 Use of improved crop varieties

To ensure increased and sustainable crop productivity, sub-Saharan Africa should focus on improved crop varieties that are adapted to diverse environments [36]. The cultivation of improved crop varieties is a strategy that can be used to enhance quality, productivity, health and nutritional value of crops. Improved varieties can also help in building crop resilience to diseases, crop pests and environmental stresses such as the emergence of new pests, water stress (including salinity changes) and heat stress. Using improved crop varieties developed to resist adverse climatic conditions will help to ensure sustained and even increased crop production despite the impacts of climate change. Additionally, varieties with improved nutritional content can reduce nutritional insecurity, thereby reducing susceptibility to diseases and improving overall health.

The use of improved crop varieties has shown to have a positive impact on the performance of smallholder farmers. A study by [36] showed that planting improved groundnut varieties in Uganda resulted in increased income by US$130–254/ha while decreasing poverty by 7–9%. These authors also reported that as the area allocated to improved maize varieties increased in Tanzania, household food security also increased while poverty declined [36]. Similarly, [37] found that the introduction of a new improved rice variety decreased poverty significantly. In a study conducted in Madagascar, [38] reported that communities that readily adopted and planted new crop varieties enjoyed higher crop yields, lower food prices, as well as higher wages for unskilled workers, greater food security and lower poverty.

6. Conclusions

It is therefore prudent to conclude that to ensure food security in Africa, especially at the household level, we need to rethink the way we produce and distribute food. The empowerment and support of small-scale farmers must be a priority. This includes improved and more inclusive agricultural extension services as well as the use of technology (such as applications) in communicating agricultural advice or climate information. The adoption of new agricultural practices is more important now than it was in the past. When small-scale farmers adopt and plant improved crop varieties they increase their agricultural income and escape poverty, thereby increasing local food security.

Several European countries already have policies and incentives that encourage diversification in farms.

Acknowledgements

We extend our utmost appreciation to Dr. Taryn Ralph for numerous discussions on this topic and initial editing of this manuscript. The authors acknowledge the Water Research Commission.

Conflict of interest

The authors declare no conflict of interest.

Author details

Samkelisiwe Nosipho Hlophe-Ginindza* and N.S. Mpandeli
Water Research Commission, Pretoria, South Africa

*Address all correspondence to: samkelisiwehg@wrc.org.za

References

[1] United Nations, Department of Economic and Social Affairs, Population Division. World population prospects: The 2015 revision, key findings and advance tables. In: Working Paper No. ESA/P/WP.241. 2015

[2] United States Department of Agriculture. Economic Research Service [Internet]. Food Security in the United States: Definitions of Hunger and Food Security. Washington: USDA; 2011

[3] High Level Panel of Experts on Food Security and Nutrition (HLPE). Investing in Smallholder Agriculture for Food Security: A Report by the High Level Panel of Experts on Food Security and Nutrition. Rome: Committee on World Food Security; 2013

[4] Global food insecurity and price increase. In: Situation Report # 1, Fiscal Year 2009. New York: United States Agency for International Development, Bureau for Democracy, Conflict, and Humanitarian Assistance, Office of US Foreign Disaster Assistance; 2009

[5] Intergovernmental Panel on Climate Change. Summary for policy makers. In: Field CB, Barros V, Stocker TF, Qin D, Dokken DJ, Ebi KL, Mastrandrea MD, Mach KJ, Plattner G-K, Allen SK, Tignor M, Midgley PM, editors. Managing the Risks of Extreme Events and Disasters to Advance Climate Change Adaptation. A Special Report of Working Groups I and II of the Intergovernmental Panel on Climate Change. Cambridge: Cambridge University Press; 2012. pp. 1-19

[6] The World Bank. Agriculture Investment Sourcebook. Washington, DC: The World Bank; 2005

[7] African Agriculture, Transformation and Outlook. NEPAD; 2013. 72 pp

[8] Statistics South Africa. Towards measuring the extent of food security in South Africa: An examination of hunger and food adequacy. In: Report No. 03-00-14. Statistics South Africa; 2019. ISBN 978-0-621-47243-1. pp. 34

[9] FAO. 2009. Available from: http://www.fao.org/fileadmin/templates/wsfs/docs/Issues_papers/HLEF2050_Global_Agriculture.pdf

[10] Cervantes-Godoy D, Dewbre J. Economic importance of agriculture for poverty reduction. In: OECD Food, Agriculture and Fisheries Working Papers. Cochran WG; 2010. p. 9 Available from: http://www.oecd.org/dataoecd/49/19/46341298.pdf. [Accessed: 15 December 2016]

[11] The State of Food Insecurity in the World 2004: Monitoring Progress Towards the World Food Summit and Millennium Development Goals. Rome: Food and Agriculture Organization; 2004

[12] Makate C, Wang R, Makate M, Mango N. Crop diversification and livelihoods of smallholder farmers in Zimbabwe: Adaptive management for environmental change. Springerplus. 2016;**5**(1):1-18

[13] Antonaci L, Demeke M, Vezzani A. The challenges of managing agricultural price and production risks in sub-Saharan Africa. In: ESA No 14-09 No. 14-9. Rome: FAO; 2014

[14] Waddington H, White H. Farmer field schools: From agricultural extension to adult education. In: Systematic Review Summary 1. London: International Initiative for Impact Evaluation (3ie); 2014

[15] AGRA. Africa Agriculture Status Report: The Business of Smallholder Agriculture in Sub-Saharan Africa (Issue 5). Nairobi, Kenya: Alliance for a Green Revolution in Africa (AGRA); 2017

[16] Anderson JR, Gershon F. Chapter 44: Agricultural Extension. In: Handbook of Agricultural Economics. Vol. 3. 2007. pp. 2343-2378

[17] Ritchie H, Roser M. 2020—"Crop Yields". Published online at OurWorldInData.org. Retrieved from: https://ourworldindata.org/crop-yields [Online Resource]

[18] Dercon S, Gilligan DO, Hoddinott J. The impact of agricultural extension and roads on poverty and consumption growth in fifteen Ethiopian villages. American Journal of Agricultural Economies. 2008;**91**(2):1007-1021

[19] De-Wit M, Stankiewicz J. Changes in surface water supply across Africa with predicted climate change. Science. 2006;**31**:1917-1921. DOI: 10.1126/science.1119929

[20] Beynon J, Akroys S, Duncan A, Jones S. Financing the Future: Options for Research and Extension in Sub-Saharan Africa. Oxford: Oxford Policy Management; 1998

[21] Thirtle C, Piesse J, Lin L. The impact of research led productivity growth on poverty in Africa, Asia and Latin America. World Development. 2003;**31**(12):1959-1975

[22] Kremen C, Iles A, Bacon C. Diversified farming systems: An agroecological, systems-based alternative to modern industrial agriculture. Ecology and Society. 2012;**17**:44

[23] Montgomery DR. Dirt: The Erosion of Civilizations. Oakland, CA, USA: University of California Press; 2012

[24] Di Falco S, Chavas JP. On crop biodiversity, risk exposure and food security in the highlands of Ethiopia. American Journal of Agricultural Economics. 2009;**91**(3):599-613

[25] Njeru EM. Crop diversification: A potential strategy to mitigate food insecurity by smallholders in sub-Saharan Africa. Journal of Agriculture, Food Systems, and Community Development. 2013;**3**(4):63-69

[26] Holling CS. Resilience and stability of ecological systems. Annual Review of Ecology and Systematics. 1973;**4**:1-23

[27] Heal G. Nature and the Marketplace: Capturing the Value of Ecosystem Services. Washington, DC: Island Press; 2000

[28] Vandermeer J, van Noordwijk M, Anderson J, Ong C, Perfecto I. Global change and multi-species agroecosystems: Concepts and issues. Agriculture, Ecosystems and Environment. 1998;**67**:1-22

[29] Gornall J, Betts R, Burke E, Clark R, Camp J, Willett K, et al. Implications of climate change for agricultural productivity in the early twenty-first century. Philosophical Transactions of the Royal Society of London. Series B, Biological Sciences. 2010;**365**(1554):2973-2989

[30] Achterbosch TJ, van Berkum S, Meijerink GW. Cash Crops and Food Security: Contributions to Income, Livelihood Risk and Agricultural Innovation. Wageningen: LEI Wageningen UR (University & Research Centre). LEI Report. 2014-2015. pp. 57

[31] Poon K, Weersink A. Factors affecting variability in farm and off-farm income. Agricultural Finance Review. 2011;**71**(3):379-397

[32] Mango N, Makate C, Mapemba L, Sopo M. The role of crop diversification in improving household food security in Central Malawi. Agriculture & Food Security. 2018;**7**:7

[33] Kalpana K. Horticultural crops value addition for nutritional security.

International Journal of Research - Granthaalayah. 2018;**6**(10):110-120

[34] Anderson JR, Gershon F. Chapter 44: Agricultural extension. In: Handbook of Agricultural Economics. Vol. 3. 2007. pp. 2343-2378

[35] Davies B, Baulcombe D, Crute I, Dunwell J, Gale M, Jones J, et al. Reaping the Benefits: Science and the Sustainable Intensification of Global Agriculture. London: The Royal Society; 2009

[36] World Bank. World Development Report 2008: Agriculture for Development. Washington, DC: World Bank; 2008

[37] Arouna A, Lokossou JC, Wopereis, MCS, Bruce-Oliver S, Roy-Macauley H. Contribution of improved rice varieties to poverty reduction and food security in subSaharan Africa. Global Food Security. 2017;**14**:54-60

[38] Dawson N, Martin A, Sikor T. Green revolution in sub-Saharan Africa: Implications of imposed innovation for the wellbeing of rural smallholders. World Development. 2016;**78**:204-218

Chapter 6

Food and Nutrition Security in East Africa (Rwanda, Burundi and South Sudan): Status, Challenges and Prospects

Michael N.I. Lokuruka

Abstract

Despite receiving international technical assistance over many years, achieving food and nutrition security has remained elusive for many developing countries. Low technological capability, inefficient production systems, increasing populations and lately climate variability, affect food production, leading to stagnation or modest gains in food and nutrition security in many nations. For many African countries, food and nutrition security continues to improve, despite the slow pace. In the East African Community, political stability, ambitious economic planning, the quest for higher agricultural productivity, improving educational achievement, sanitation and health, are contributing to improving food and nutrition security. To support the process, Rwanda, established Vision 2020, while Burundi and South Sudan have yet to develop plans for a coherent development blueprint. The blue prints of the Member States bore Vision 2050 for the East African Community and Vision 2063 for the African Union. This chapter examines the status of food and nutrition security in Rwanda, Burundi and South Sudan. It gives country-specific recommendations for achieving it-including investment in agriculture and agribusiness, value addition of agricultural commodities, decelerating population growth, using adaptive research to solve farmer-problems, strengthening farmer-organizations and integrating variables that influence food and nutrition security achievement.

Keywords: Rwanda, Burundi, South Sudan, economic and social development, agriculture, food and nutrition security, status, challenges, prospects

1. Introduction

This Chapter examines the food security situation in Rwanda, Burundi and South Sudan. Each country is discussed in terms of economic growth, social and development indicators, and its outlook for food and nutrition security attainment. However, this chapter is best read with chapter 1 as the geography, environmental, weather and related issues are addressed in chapter 1 for the region as a whole, including the three countries discussed in this Chapter.

The thesis concludes with an examination of the encompassing strategies that are likely to improve the overall food and nutrition security situation of the EAC block, as a unit, rather than as Individual Member States.

2. RWANDA

2.1 Economy, agriculture and social development

Rwanda with a population of about 12 million people experienced an economic growth rate of about 8% for the decade 2000–2010 [1]. The political stability and impressive economic growth that the country has experienced since the end of the civil war, has encouraged growth in the country's population. Food production also continues to benefit from both the stable and growing economy and population increase, especially of skilled labour. However, the rapid growth rate in the human population is undesirable, especially for the rural, agrarian and poor households, who also tend to bear a proportionately higher number of children than their urban counterparts. Rwanda embarked on Vision 2020 immediately from 1997 as it aimed at transforming itself into a middle income country by 2020 based on a knowledge-based economy and service-oriented sectoral growth [2]. Clearly defined, "Vision 2020," seeks to transform the country from a low-income, agriculture-based economy to a knowledge-based, service-oriented economy with middle-income country status by 2020. The goal aims to achieve rapid development sustained by the high economic growth, leading to poverty reduction and reduced inequality. From 2001 to 2015, the growth in real GDP averaged about 8% per annum [3]. Substantial improvements in living standards, a two-thirds drop in child mortality and near universal primary school enrollment are the result of stability, good economic planning and strong economic growth [4]. Despite the impressive achievements, Rwanda is a small, land-locked country in Sub-Saharan Africa that is part of the EAC, but can also pass for a country in Central Africa. It has the highest population density in Sub-Saharan Africa and is one of the poorest countries in the World, with about 47% of its population living on less than US $1.25/day [5]. Agriculture accounts for 29.5% of GDP, 45.9% of employment, 63% of foreign exchange earnings, and meets about 90% of the country's food needs [5]. The majority of Rwandan farmers practice subsistence farming on small, hilly plots that are characterized by very low productivity. Up to half of the country's arable land is severely degraded, due to overuse and soil erosion, and, has low soil fertility. The country's agriculture relies on the application of insignificant amounts of pesticides, fertilizers and improved seeds [5]. Despite the above, Rwanda ranks the 123rd out of 157 countries in progress to meet the SDGs [6]. According to the most recent Rwanda Demographic Household Survey of 2015, the infant mortality rate is 32 per 1000 live births, with an under-5 mortality rate of 50 infants per 1000 live births [7].

The country launched the Crop Intensification Programme and Policy in 2007 in its quest for increasing food production, leading to improved output of beans, potatoes and cassava [8]. The Maputo Declaration of 2003 [9], in which African countries were advised to spend a minimum of 10% of their GDP on agriculture and food production, led Rwanda to adopt the Crop Intensification Programme, with the above results. Although it did not meet the 10% requirement, all indications are that it is on its way to achieve it.

2.2 Food and nutrition security

Despite the impressive achievement and commitment from the Government of Rwanda (GoR), food and nutrition insecurity still lingers in the general population. There are differences between the various poverty and nutrition indicators among the Provinces and in the Districts. The food and nutrition security indicators show that about 48.7 and 22.1% of the rural and urban populations, respectively, are still food and nutrition insecure [10]. The poor rural households can typically be described to be living in crowded homes, relying on low income agriculture and poorly paid casual labour. They farm small plots of less than 0.5 hectares on steep slopes of infertile soils. Most of the children in the rural household are stunted and come from lowly educated or illiterate households. In rural Rwanda's poorest District of Nyamagabe, 73% of the population lives below the international poverty line of US$1.90/day. The Gini coefficient for the country was 0.45 and 0.49 in 2002/2003 and 2010/2011 FY, respectively [11].

In part due to low agricultural productivity, over a third of the Rwandan population normally experiences food insecurity and under-nutrition, despite Rwanda's impressive economic growth. Nationally, 38% of children under-5 years are stunted and 2% suffer from acute malnutrition. Stunting in children increases with the child's age up until 23 months and rises from 18% in children of 6–8 months of age and peaks at 49% in children who are 18–23 months old. The nutritional status of children varies by Province, with stunting being highest in the Western Province at 45% but is lowest in the city of Kigali at 23%. Rural children have a 41% stunting rate compared to 24% in urban children. A mother's level of education and wealth quartile have been shown to vary inversely with the prevalence of stunting; the prevalence of stunting is lowest in children in poor households at 21% but is higher in children living in the poorest households at 49%. The prevalence of stunting is lowest in children whose mothers have a secondary education or higher (19%) but is higher in those children whose mothers' have no education (47%) [7].

By the age of 19, about 21% of adolescent girls had begun childbearing in Rwanda in 2014–2015, which was a slight increase from 20% in 2010 and this seems to contribute to malnutrition in children born to such young mothers [7, 12]. Adolescent girls who are likely to be malnourished run the risk of a having a low birth-weight baby, who will likely become malnourished, and, be at increased risk of illness and death than babies born to older mothers. It has also been established that the risk of stunting is 33% higher among first-born children of girls under 18 years of age in Sub-Saharan Africa, such that early motherhood appears to be a key driver of malnutrition [13]. Rwanda similar to other rising economies is also experiencing the double burden of malnutrition, with 21% of women and 8% of children under-5 years suffering from overweight and obesity [7]. Eighty percent of all households are food secure, with 4% considered marginally food secure and 0.5–0.6% severely food insecure. In the livelihood zones of Western Congo Nile Crest Tea Zone, Lake Kivu Coffee Zone and the Northern Highland Beans and Wheat Zone, the poverty indices are 49, 37 and 32%, respectively [5]. Therefore the level of food insecurity is particularly high in the western and northern parts of the country. Among Provinces, Western Province has over 35% of its households considered as food insecure. Fourty-two percent of all severely food-insecure households in Rwanda are found in the Western Province, despite having 22% of the country's households. The National Institute of Statistics of Rwanda avers that Rutsiro, Nyamagabe, Nyabihu, Nyaruguru, Rusizi Karongi and Nyamasheke Districts have 57%, 42%, 39%, 37%, 36%, 35%, and 35% households that are classified as food insecure, respectively [14]. Under-nutrition, especially stunting in children, is attributed not only to food insecurity and poverty, but also to inadequate feeding, particularly poor complementary feeding practices. Estimates show that only 19% of Rwandan children of 6–23 months age receive a minimum acceptable diet [7].

2.3 Prospects

Rwanda is faced with the challenge of an increasing population, which in turn impacts negatively on the per capita food production, availability and consumption.

The increasing population requires land to build homes on, while road and rail infrastructure, industries, institutions and other social amenities also require land. The fixed amount of land available for these competing needs means that the arable land sizes will keep reducing and the chances of hunger, malnutrition and under-nourishment may increase due to reduced food production. Rwanda's "Feed the Future" Multi-Year Strategy identified market linkages, infrastructure, nutrition, innovation, and policy as focal points for support and intervention, making it multi-sectoral in order to make the strategy effective. Rwanda engaged development partners in order to revise the national food and nutrition policy and linked it with its 2013–2018 strategic plan, and the Comprehensive Africa Agriculture Development Programme [15]. This approach should bear fruit in a few years ahead. Climate variability has impacted on the country's agriculture, similar to the situation in the other member states of the EAC, with the potential for a rise in food and nutrition insecurity, both in the short and long-term. But the proportion of the food and nutrition insecure population in Rwanda will still be lower than in food-deficient countries like Burundi and Kenya.

2.4 Recommendations

The country should:

- Identify multi-sectoral approaches and coordination efforts as key ingredients to accelerate progress in nutrition and food security programmes. The GoR having created a national early childhood development (ECD) program to have a family-focused approach to address child stunting in Rwanda, it is envisioned that the coordination secretariat and the ECD program will complement each other and accelerate Rwanda's food security and nutrition agenda

- Develop a new policy, focussed on integrated nutrition interventions that involve multi-sectoral management to prevent of all forms of malnutrition among women and children and make it effective

- Develop a strategy that focuses on enabling improvements for private-sector-led growth in the agriculture sector and on building capacity within value chains to improve the competitiveness of farmers and commodities

- Discourage through social education, early child bearing as it contributes to malnutrition, with serious consequences for maternal health, baby development and growth

- Concentrate its food security improvement interventions in Western Province as more than 42% of all severely food insecure households in Rwanda are found there

3. Burundi

3.1 Economy, agriculture and social development

Burundi is a land locked State in Central Africa and is one of the most densely populated countries on the continent, with 470 inhabitants per square kilometre. Its economy is heavily reliant on agriculture, which, despite the paucity of arable land, employs 80% of the population. Poverty is mainly rural and overwhelmingly affects small-holder farmers. Burundi is the second most densely populated country in Africa and the 5th poorest country in the world [16]. It has a population of about 11 million people with a birth rate of 6 children per woman of child-bearing age. The high population growth rate contributes significantly to its high poverty index and low scores on all food and nutrition indicators. The IMF has classified Burundi as having the highest level of poverty and worst health indicators in the EAC [17]. The country experienced unprecedented food and nutrition insecurity between 1993 and 2005 due to the breakout of the civil war [18], and again from 2015 to 2018 due to the political instability resulting from the extension of the term of the Presidency beyond the legislated two terms of 5 years each [19].

Most of the Burundian population lives in abject poverty, especially in rural areas. The level of food insecurity is almost twice as high as the average for sub-Saharan African countries, as was shown by 1.8 million people needing humanitarian assistance in 2018 according to the Humanitarian Response Plan [20]. Agriculture contributes 40% of the country's GDP and is the main source of employment for 80% of the country's population, despite not being able to generate adequate income.

Less than 5% of the country's population has access to electricity. While access to safe drinking water and sanitation remains very low, only about 52.1% of rural households and 2% of rural households have access to electricity [21]. Between 2010 and 2017, Burundi experienced a remarkable decline in fertility, which fell from 6.4 to 5.5 children per woman on average, thus slowing its population growth.

The economy is recovering slowly, with growth reaching about 1.6% in 2018 compared to 0.5% in 2017, after two consecutive years of recession in 2015 (−3.9%) and 2016 (−0.6%) [22]. The economy faces a fragile recovery that remains below the 4.2% recorded from 2004 to 2014 and many challenges including: a lack of budgetary resources to finance public investments, a persistent shortage of foreign exchange with falling international reserves, a vulnerable financial sector and increasing fiscal and current deficits.

In order to prevent and control the spread of Ebola, Burundi has set up screening and treatment centres at various points along its border with the neighbouring Democratic Republic of Congo (DRC), with assistance from the World Bank. Despite recording fewer COVID-19 cases and deaths than other EAC Member States except South Sudan by the 27th April, 2020, it is likely to go into deep recession due to its fragile economy and the high dependence on other member States of the EAC trading bloc for its imports and exports.

3.2 Food and nutrition security

Malnutrition in childhood and pregnancy has many adverse consequences for child survival and long-term well-being. Malnutrition also has far-reaching consequences for human capital, economic productivity, and overall national development. According to the findings of the 2016–2017 Demographic and Health Survey, the country has a chronic malnutrition rate of 56%, one of the highest in the World. Malnutrition affects over 1 million children under 5 years of age [23]. The expected increase in the population to 15.3 million by 2030 and its doubling to 23.5 million by 2050, spells disaster for Burundi [22]. Furthermore, eighty-eight percent of the country's population resides in rural areas and 45% of the country's population is under 15 years of age [24]. While the level of poverty in Sub-Saharan Africa has reduced overall, the level of poverty in Burundi has stagnated. As of 2016, 78% of the population lived on less than US$1.90 a day [24, 25]. Ninety percent of the population depends on agriculture and poverty disproportionately affects rural farmers [24]. Currently, Burundi ranks 132nd out of 157 countries in terms of progress toward meeting the SDGs [25]. According to the most recent data, the maternal mortality ratio is 712 per 100,000 live births, 27% of female deaths are related to pregnancy or childbearing, and one in 13 children will die before reaching 5 years of age. Burundi's nutrition and food security situation has been adversely affected by the ongoing conflict and political instability, in addition to the recurrent natural disasters and epidemics. Burundi ranked last on the Global Hunger Index (GHI) in 2014 [26]. Approximately 2.6 million people were projected to be food insecure as of October 2017 and recent Famine Early Warning Systems Network (FEWS NET) 2018 estimates did not show any improvement [27]. The food security situation remained stressed through May 2018, with some poor households reaching crisis level of food insecurity [27]. Burundi's child stunting prevalence of 56% is among the highest in the world, with levels among the under-5 s having dropped by only 2 percentage points between 2010 and 2017. Also between 2010 and 2017, underweight and wasting prevalence remained virtually unchanged. Rural areas have a much higher prevalence of stunting than urban areas, at 59 and 28%, respectively. Following this pattern, Bujumbura Mairie, the most urban of the Provinces, has the lowest prevalence of stunting at 24%. In the rest of the country, which is highly rural, stunting prevalence varies from 49% in Bururi to 66% in Muyinga [23]. It has been established that stunting levels are linked to maternal education and wealth levels, as 40% of children whose mothers have secondary education or higher are stunted, while the prevalence rises to 61% of children whose mothers had no formal education. According to the wealth status of the mother, 31% of children in the highest wealth quartile are stunted, while in the lowest wealth quartile, 69% are stunted. In Burundi, the level of stunting increases with age, such that 36% of children 6–8 months old are stunted. The prevalence of stunting steadily increases in children and peaks at 66% among children aged 36–47 months. The high prevalence of stunting among children 36–47 months old may be a result of the early cessation of exclusive breastfeeding and inadequate complementary feeding of children 6–23 months of age [23]. The prevalence of exclusive breastfeeding drops dramatically among children 4–5 months old, such that 64% of these children are exclusively breastfed, while among those aged 1 day-3 months, the prevalence of exclusive breastfeeding is 93% [23]. The change to complimentary feeding puts children at risk of exposure to disease-causing agents that are transmitted through unsafe water and unhygienic food handling practices, which can lead to an increase in recurring infections and exacerbate malnutrition. In Burundi childbearing begins early, such that by the age of 19, twenty nine percent of adolescent girls had begun childbearing in 2016–2017, which is a slight decrease from 31 percent in 2010 [23, 28]. In Sub-Saharan Africa, the risk of stunting is 33% higher among first-born children of mothers under 18 years. Early child-bearing has been shown to be a key causative factor of malnutrition [28], because, relative to older mothers, adolescent girls are more likely to be malnourished and have a low birth-weight baby who is more likely to become malnourished, and be at increased risk of illness and death, than those born to older mothers [28]. The prevalence of anaemia among women of reproductive age and adolescent girls increased dramatically from 45 and 19%, in 2010 and 2016–2017, to 61% and 39%, in 2010 and 2016–2017, respectively. This further increases the risk of low birth weight that also contributes to child stunting. While 75% of the country's population has access to an improved water source, 95% do not treat their drinking water, thus posing a challenge to improvements in WASH. Only 34% of Burundians have access to an improved toilet, with 56% using non-slab or open latrines. These practices, coupled with flooding, increase the risk of disease. Burundi has suffered from recurrent cholera and malaria outbreaks, which can exacerbate ill-health and malnutrition. As of October 2017, there were more than 6.6 million cases of malaria in the country [26]. While recurrent infection contributes to high levels of chronic malnutrition, it also impacts on acute malnutrition. A half of Burundi's 18 Provinces have malnutrition levels of 5–9%, which is categorized as acute. In the Provinces, the wasting rates are 74, 74 and 81% in Kirundo, Kayanza, and Karusi, respectively. Malaria, diarrhea, and poor diet quality all contribute to acute malnutrition in the country [29].

3.3 Prospects

Approximately 80% of the country's 11 million people live below the poverty line of US $1.25/day [25]. The general drivers of food and nutrition insecurity for the country include an unplanned increasing population, improper use and sometimes, non-use of the available land for food production and when the two factors are combined, falling food production results.

Political stability is a prerequisite to long-term economic development of the country and therefore improvements in food production and long-term and sustained fall in food and nutrition insecurity. Infrastructure improvements, market access to the EAC markets, especially for its livestock, may assist in opening up the country to regional trade and contribute to cash inflows from the partner states of the EAC. However, its situation remains bleak in the face of political instability in the short term, low economic growth potential and unwillingness to fully integrate into the EAC. The stagnating rate of reduction in stunting and wasting will linger on for quite some time into the future, more so due to the significant population increase, despite any potential economic growth. Any improvements in food and nutrition security will still be low as the arable land will compete for land for housing, infrastructure, industry and institutions.

Depending on the extent of infection of the population by the COVID-19 pandemic and the level of control and management by government, the expected disruption to the already fragile Burundian economy is bound to have disastrous consequences on food security, nutrition and health indices.

3.4 Recommendations

The Government should endeavour to:

- Reduce unplanned population increases
- Reduce the malarial, diarrhea, and poor diet influence as they impact malnutrition
- Improve access to safe water while improving food handling and hygiene practices
- Continue with the education of communities on the negative influence of early childbearing on child health, nutritional status and child growth and development
- Target rural farmers as poverty disproportionately affects them
- Discourage the early cessation of exclusive breastfeeding through appropriate maternal education, and by improving the adequacy of complementary feeding of children 6–23 months of age
- Work on reducing underweight and wasting prevalence in the rural areas

- Join International peace building efforts to stop the ongoing conflict especially with the rebels operating from the DRC and for the restoration of political stability
- Partner with the international community to realize political stability as a prerequisite to economic growth, international trade and integration into the EAC

4. Republic of South Sudan

4.1 Political, economic and social situation

South Sudan has a population of about 12 million people [30]. It has suffered ethnic violence and has been in a civil war since 2013, only two years after gaining its independence from Sudan.

Its weather is tropical and is characterized by a rainy season of high humidity and large amounts of rainfall, followed by a drier season. July tends to be the coolest month with average temperatures falling between 20 and 30°C, while March is the warmest month with average temperatures ranging from 23 to 37°C. Much of the annual rainfall comes between May and October, though rainy season sometimes commences in April and extends to November [30], thus making May the wettest month. The country's weather is "influenced by the annual shift of the Inter-Tropical Zone and the shift to southerly and southwesterly winds" leading to slightly lower environmental temperatures, higher humidity and heavy cloud cover [30].

South Sudan has a predominantly rural and subsistence economy. The region has been negatively affected by war since 1956, resulting in low infrastructure development, and major properties' destruction and displacements of populations. More than 2 million people are reported to have died, and, more than 4 million are internally displaced persons, or have become refugees as a result of the civil war [30]. It is estimated that there are more than 1.5 million persons out of the country. Improved education is needed to pave the way for greater economic opportunities and reduce South Sudan's reliance on oil and gas. South Sudan's recovering education system still faces many challenges, which are exacerbated by famine and the ongoing violence [31], in addition to the poor infrastructure, lack of qualified teaching and administrative staff and amenities in schools, etc.

4.2 Food and nutrition security

South Sudan has a cyclical food security situation that is typical of a tropical country with a rainy and a dry season. The ongoing conflict has also altered the natural dynamics and has made the implementation of the usual coping strategies difficult. Food shortages disappear or reduce substantially, depending on the State, after the rainy season and during harvest. In the following dry season, food shortages are evident requiring some assistance to fill the food security gaps.

Since the ongoing conflict started in 2013, the food and nutrition security situation has remained at the most compromised level. The combination of conflict, economic crisis and lack of adequate levels of agricultural production has eroded vulnerable households' ability to cope. This situation is evident as described in the chapters that follow despite the efforts of international humanitarian agencies to try to manage the situation and bring it under control. The efforts between 2015 and 2019 are described below.

By September 2015, approximately 3.9 million people–nearly one in every three Sudanese, were severely food insecure and 3.6 million were considered to be 'stressed' [31]. An estimated 30,000 people were facing catastrophic food insecurity (IPC Level 5) in Unity State, leading to destitution, starvation, and death for some [32]. At the height of the lean season in July 2016, some 4.8 million people–more than one in every four people in South Sudan–were estimated to be severely food insecure. This number rose to about five million in 2017. More than one million children under age 5 were estimated to be acutely malnourished, including more than 273,600 who were severely malnourished in 2016 [33]. As of January 2017, 3.8 million were estimated to be in IPC 3-IPC 5, meaning that they were anywhere between crisis and catastrophe status of food insecurity. This was such that a month later, the number of people in need of humanitarian assistance (IPC 3 and above) had increased to almost 5 million, out of which 100,000 were facing famine conditions. As a result, famine was declared in Leer and Mayendit Counties of Greater Unity State, Koch County and parts of Panyijiar County [34]. By mid-2017, an estimated 50% of the country's population was declared to be severely food insecure compared to 45% of the population a few months earlier. This was apparently the greatest number of people ever to experience severe food insecurity (IPC 3–5) in South Sudan from 2013. Immediate and sustained multi-sectoral humanitarian assistance was delivered to the affected population in the rest of the year. However, some 45,000 people in Leer, Koch, Mayendit in former Unity State and Ayod County in former Jonglei were reported to be in IPC 5 status of food insecurity as a result of the continued armed conflict, food shortages associated with seasonality and humanitarian assistance delivery constraints. In the Greater Jonglei State, food security rapidly deteriorated in the same period, predominantly in the counties of Ayod, Canal/Pigi, Duk, Nyirol and Uror, which faced Emergency (IPC 4) acute food insecurity, with Ayod having an estimated 20,000 people experiencing Humanitarian Catastrophe (IPC 5) through to July 2017 [35]. Due to the catastrophic nature of the situation between July and Dec 2017 [36], WFP resumed the integrated rapid response mechanism and deployed teams in Bilkey, Nyandit, Kurwai, Jaibor, Chuil, Buot and Ulang, providing life-saving food and nutrition assistance to over 96,600 people, including over 17,000 children under the age of five. For the period of January–September 2018, an estimated 48% of the population faced Crisis Level (IPC 3) or worse acute food insecurity, despite the harvest and the continued large-scale assistance that was being provided [37, 38]. By September 2018, 59% of the total population was estimated to be variously facing crisis to catastrophe levels of food insecurity. However, as is normal in the post-harvest period October–December of 2018, the number of people in need of humanitarian assistance reduced (to about 43% of the total population), although over 20,000 still experienced catastrophe conditions and extreme food gaps. In early 2019, 49% of the total population faced acute food insecurity, with over 36,000 people in catastrophic conditions (IPC 5) [39].

In the period January –December 2019, and with the availability of humanitarian food assistance, the situation that was experienced in 2018 over the same period was evident, with over 57% of the population facing acute food insecurity, while over 45,000 people were estimated to be in catastrophe phase of food insecurity [41]. The situation in South Sudan may be similar in 2020 or worse than it was in 2019 due to the uncertainties and the high cost of containment of the COVID-19 pandemic.

The situation described above for South Sudan is both depressing and concerning and points to the need for the International Community to do all in its power to bring the civil war to an end, so that some level of normalcy returns to the country. From the above estimates, some 45–60% of citizens of South Sudan can access food and are able to recover their food security situation after harvest in any year, while 50–60% faces food insecurity of various levels in the dry season, but with less than 1% in catastrophe status (IPC 5).

4.3 Prospects

The food security and nutrition situation in South Sudan has been deteriorating in recent years due to the outbreak of conflicts, below par food production, disruption of markets and trade, hyper-inflation, diseases and natural disasters such as floods and drought in parts of the country. With the ongoing macroeconomic crisis including the rapid depreciation of the South Sudanese Pound, hyper-inflation and the surge in food prices, urban food insecurity remains a grave concern. To illustrate the point, an assessment was conducted in Juba urban areas (including Kator, Juba town, and Munuki) in September 2017, to understand the food security and nutrition status of the urban population, comprising some 1371 households. The survey provided representative estimates of key food security and nutrition indicators for the Juba urban population as well as each of the three blocks within the greater Juba urban area.

The key findings of the assessment were [40]:

- Overall, food insecurity affected 76% of the households surveyed. Among them 21% were severely food insecure and 55% being moderately food insecure. This showed a significant deterioration of the situation from September 2016, when 51% of the population was food insecure.

- Fifty one percent of the households were reported to experience poor food consumption, with 28% on the borderline and only 21% having what would be regarded an acceptable level of food consumption.

- Nearly three-fourth of the households were in a moderate to severe hunger scale (59% moderate and 14% severe).

- Overall, the prevalence of Global Acute Malnutrition was 10.1% (classified as serious by the WHO), a figure that is similar to that seen in the assessments done in 2015 (12.2%) and 2016 (11.2%).

- Nearly 46% of respondents reported spending an amount of 65–75% or greater of their total household expenditure on food, thus indicating economic vulnerability and poor access to food.

- The Juba urban population accesses food mainly from the public markets, with about 93% of households reporting markets as their primary source for cereals and only 8% of the population reported cultivating, while a tiny 2% owned livestock.

- The percentage of households adopting crisis and emergency strategies to achieve food security was 23 and 35%, respectively

    - It was established that most households got their drinking water from unsafe sources such as rivers (69%) and surface reservours (31%)

- In terms of toilet use, 69, 16, 6 and 9% of households used open pit traditional latrine, water-seal latrine, flush toilet and open bush, respectively.

- Results indicate worsening household food consumption and nutrition for Juba residents thus driving households to apply severe coping strategies. This seems to be driven by currency depreciation (72%), high food prices (69%) and violence (50%).

- The food insecurity situation in the three blocks of greater Juba urban area was 67% in Juba town, and 84% and 79% in Kator and Munuki peri-urban areas, respectively.

The situation in the greater Juba area should apply to most parts of the country as the conflict and other socio-political factors remain similar. Lack of extension services, certified seeds and other inputs compound food and nutrition security attainment in rural areas.

4.4 Recommendations

The Government of South Sudan (GoSS) and its partners should:

- Endeavour to stop the continuing economic crisis and hyperinflation amidst stagnant or falling income levels of market-dependent households.

- Integrate vulnerable households into programmes that aim to raise their food and nutrition security situation

- Reduce the adoption of disruptive and non-reversible coping mechanisms which result in detrimental effects on future household productivity and ability to stand up to shocks. Programmes targeting the most vulnerable households to build their resilience should be prioritized

- Deliver relief while further scaling up the social transfers to the poor and most vulnerable segments of the population

- Continue scaling up programmes for the treatment of malnutrition as well as the application of the common public health measures such as vaccination, deworming, supplementation and improvement of water and sanitation. Disease prevention is crucial for the improvement of the nutrition situation given that findings showed that incidence of diarrhoea was related to child malnutrition

- Endeavour to maintain the current peace and reconciliation so that the disruption of livelihoods stops, in a country that has probably the most promising future based on the considerable petroleum and gas deposits, rich agricultural soils, and, the highest forest cover in all of East Africa.

Due to lack of data on malnutrition is South Sudan, the estimates for 2020 give the stunting rate for the under-5 s as 31.3%, while wasting for the same age group is 24.3% [41]. The percent of children 6–24 months of age that are breastfed is 45.6%, which is lower than the East African Region level of 59.7%. The data on birth weights, poverty level and under-nutrition is lacking. However, iron deficiency anemia in women is estimated as 34%. The above data was obtained by modeling by UNICEF/World Bank group [41].

In conclusion, the formation of a Government of National Unity by President Salva Kiir and his nemesis Dr. Riek Machar is critical as they work towards ending the conflict, reducing the suffering of the general population, and, allowing peace to prevail for the country to plan its development path.

5. General conclusions and recommendations on improving food and nutrition security in the EAC

The EAC is continuing with the adoption of strategies and technologies that increase agricultural productivity in order to achieve higher yields of the staple crops, as the increasing human populations are likely to erode any gains made in food production. The focus is on rural areas where agriculture is often the only means of livelihood and where poverty is much higher than the urban areas. To achieve improved food production requires adequate water, either through rainfall or from underground sources, and in addition arable land, fertilizers and other inputs. In addition, the use of farm machinery and other technological solutions can result in higher efficiency rather than relying on the inefficient hoes and oxen for land preparation.

Modern practices that lead to a flourishing agriculture sector in any country are a result of continuous, application-oriented research and development. The key to success in this regard lies in the two-way flow of information between researchers and farmers. By using extension services, problems faced by farmers can be reported to researchers for possible solutions, and where solutions are available, they are transmitted to the field for trial and subsequent adoption, where they seem to work. The application in China and the United Arab Emirates of such strategic food security measures are lessons member states of the EAC can pick and implement.

Governments should also ensure that the food in their countries is available, accessible, and for people who do not produce enough food, having enough income to buy food in order to realize improved food and nutrition security.

Rained agriculture is no longer reliable in the face of climate variability. This calls for the use of irrigation `and smart agricultural practices for reliable food production. It is imperative that member states of the EAC adopt efficient systems of irrigation. Better storage systems that maintain premium quality of produce, reduce losses and food wastage through the application of cost-effective and appropriate food preservation technologies, are necessary.

It is critical that financial institutions ensure that credit facilities and related support services are accessible to farmers. As banks may often not understand agriculture due to the risks associated with uncertainties in weather, etc., the formation of farmer-cooperatives can enable members to access credit with relative ease. In order to make agriculture more efficient, it is necessary to invest in technology. Agriculture should be conducted as a business. This requires better management of finances and record keeping as doing that will attract financial institutions that can lend to farmers. This is an important role that governments can take up, if they require better performance of the agriculture sector. Credit is important for the sector to transit from subsistence to commercial farming. The formation of farmer-cooperatives can help farmers to access credit easily, as Cooperatives act as guarantors to make sure that the money is paid back at the time agreed with the lending institutions. The trust that can be developed with banks can open the way for farmers to borrow money from banks, who may trust cooperatives more than individual farmers. As part of the efforts to improve food and nutrition security, Governments require to encourage stakeholders in the supply chain to focus on agriculture as a business and invest in it. The Vision 2063 of the African Union resonates with the Vision 2050 of the EAC on the attainment of food and nutrition security in the trading bloc.

In conclusion, Science, Technology and Innovation should benefit the agriculture sector through the use of improved and high yielding seed varieties, new ways of tackling climate change, and offering appropriate technologies if the sector has to contribute significantly to the growth of the regional economy and improve food and nutrition security in the member states. However, the breakout of the novel COVID-19 pandemic in early 2020 in the EAC is bound to result in slowed economic growth for most of the member states, depending on the severity of the infection in the Member State, the extent of interruption of economic activities and the application of economically disruptive measures for the containment purposes aimed at stemming the spread of the virus across the region. Also, the desert locust invasion in the region beginning June 2019 and which became severe in 2020, especially in the semi-arid and arid regions of Kenya, will undoubtedly reduce food production and lead to the worsening of food and nutrition security for the region, with Kenya, the southwestern part of South Sudan and probably Karamoja in Uganda likely to experience worrisome situations. However, as recovery efforts from the pandemic continue, Tanzania is predicted to record the highest economic growth in the region for FY 2019/2020 and 2020/2021, with Kenya being more resilient than either Uganda or Rwanda, despite recording the highest number of COVID-9 cases and bearing the heaviest brunt of the desert locust invasion. The generally good economic situation is buoyed by favourable weather and therefore a plentiful food supply, low oil/energy cost, and a generally low inflation rate. South Sudan, unfortunately, due to the continuing civil war and the pandemic will remain the weakest economy in the region for a few years to come.

Acronyms

DRC	Democratic Republic of Congo
EAC	East African Community
ECD	Early Childhood Development Programme
FEWS NET	Famine Early Warning Systems Network
FY	Financial Year
GDP	Gross Domestic Product
GoR	Government of Rwanda
GoSS	Government of South Sudan
IMF	International Monetary Fund
IPC	Integrated Food Security Phase Classification
SDGs	Sustainable Development Goals
UNICEF	United Nations Children's Fund
USAID	United States Agency for International Development
UN OCHA	United Nations Office for the Coordination of Humanitarian Affairs
WASH	Water Sanitation and Hygiene
WHO	World Health Organization

Author details

Michael N.I. Lokuruka
Department of Food Science, Nutrition and Technology, Karatina University,
Box 1957-10101, Karatina, Kenya

*Address all correspondence to: mlokuruka@gmail.com; mlokuruka@karu.ac.ke

References

[1] Malunda Dickson. 2012. Rwanda Study Case of Economic Transformation-Report for the African Centre for Economic Transformation (ACET). Institute of Policy Analysis and Research (IPAR), Rwanda, Kigali, March 2012.

[2] Republic of Rwanda. Rwanda Vision 2020. 2000. Ministry of Finance and Economic Planning, Kigali, Rwanda.

[3] USAID. 2017. "Country Profile: Rwanda." Available at: https://feedthefuture.gov/country/rwanda.

[4] UNICEF. 2017. The State of the World's Children 2017. Available at: https://www.unicef.org/sowc/html. Accessed on 10th March, 2020.

[5] World Bank. 2017. Rwanda poverty assessment. Found at: http://documents.worldbank.org/curated/en/255161467998828941/pdf/100631-WP-P124629-PUBLIC-Box393238B-Rwanda-Poverty-Assessment-Final.pdf. Accessed on 19th Apr 2020.

[6] Sachs, J., Schmidt-Traub, G., Kroll, C., Durand-Delacre, D. and Teksoz, K. 2017. SDG Index and Dashboards Report 2017. New York, NY.

[7] National Institute of Statistics of Rwanda (NISR), Ministry of Health-MOH-Rwanda and ICF International. 2015. Rwanda Demographic and Health Survey 2010. NISR, MoH and ICF International, Kigali, Rwanda.

[8] Nicola Cantore. 2010. The Crop Intensification Program in Rwanda-a Sustainability Analysis. UNEP/UNDP/ODI, London. Found at: https://www.odi.org/sites/odi.org.uk/files/odi-assets/publications-opinion-files/7094.pdf. Accessed on 19th Apr 2020.

[9] AUDA-NEPAD. 2019. AU 2003 Maputo Declaration on Agriculture and Food Security. Maputo, Mozambique found at: https://www.nepad.org/caadp/publication/au-2003-maputo-declaration-agriculture-and-food-security. Accessed on 19th Apr 2020.

[10] FAO. 2018. Hunger and Food Security, Rwanda. FAOSTAT, Rome. Found at: http://www.fao.org/faostat/en/#country/184. Accessed on 19th Apr 2020.

[11] World Bank. 2013. Gini Index (World Bank estimate) for Rwanda. Found at: https://data.worldbank.org/indicator/SI.POV.GINI?locations=RW-BO-FI-DK-NO-SE&start=1997&end=2014. Accessed on 19th Apr 2020.

[12] NISR, MOH, and ICF. 2010. Rwanda Demographic and Health Survey 2010. 2010. NISR, MOH, and ICF International, Calverton, Maryland, USA.

[13] Fink, G., Sudfeld, C.R., Danaei, G., Ezzati, M., and Fawzi, W.W. 2014. "Scaling-Up Access to Family Planning May Improve Linear Growth and Child Development in Low and Middle-Income Countries." PLoS ONE 9(7): e102391. Doi: 10.1371/journal.pone.0102391.

[14] National Institute of Statistics of Rwanda-NISR-Rwanda, Ministry of Agriculture-MOA-Rwanda and World Food Programme. 2015. NISR, MOA, and WFP. "Rwanda 2015": Comprehensive food security and vulnerability analysis.

[15] New Partnership for Africa's Development (NEPAD). 2009. "Signed Comprehensive Africa Agriculture Development Programme (CAADP) Compact." Available at: http://www.nepad.org/sites/default/files/Nigeria-Signed-Compact.pdf. Accessed on 17th Apr 2020.

[16] USAID. 2017. Food Assistance Fact Sheet–Burundi. Available at: https://www.usaid.gov/burundi/food-assistance. Accessed on 19th Apr 2020.

[17] IMF. 2007. Burundi poverty reduction strategy paper; IMF Country report No. 07/46, IMF Publication services, Feb 2007. Washington, DC.

[18] AU/UN Peacemaker. 2000. Arusha peace and reconciliation agreement for Burundi. 2000. UN peacemaker/AU. Found at: https://peacemaker.un.org/sites/peacemaker.un.org/files/BI_000828_Arusha%20Peace%20and%

[19] Reconciliation%20Agreement%20for%20Burundi.pdf. Accessed on 20th Apr 2020.

[20] World Bank. 2019. Burundi, access to electricity rural. Found at: https://tradingeconomics.com/burundi/access-to-electricity-rural-percent-of-rural-population-wb-data.html. Accessed on 20th Apr 2020.

[21] Population Reference Bureau. 2017. "2017 World Population Data Sheet." Available at: http://www.prb.org/pdf17/2017_World_Population.pdf. Accede on 6th Apr 2020.

[22] ISTEEBU, Ministère de la Santé Publique et de la Lutte contre le Sida [Burundi] (MSPLS), and ICF International 2012. Enquête Démographique et de Santé Burundi 2010. ISTEEBU, MSPLS and ICF International.

[23] World Bank. 2017. "Burundi Country Overview." Available at: https://www.worldbank.org/en/country/burundi/overview. Accessed on 6th March 2020.

[24] Sachs, J., Schmidt-Traub, G., Kroll, C., Durand-Delacre, D. and Teksoz, K. 2017. SDG Index and Dashboards Report 2017. New York: Bertelsmann Stiftung and Sustainable Development Solutions Network (SDSN).

[25] Global Hunger Index (GHI). 2017. Global Hunger Index Results: Global, Regional, and National Trends=Burundi. Available at: http://www.globalhungerindex.org/results-2017/. Accessed on 10th Apr 2020.

[26] FEWS NET. 2017. Burundi Remote Monitoring Update. Available at: https://reliefweb.int/sites/reliefweb.int/files/resources/Burundi_December%20 2017_%20RMU_%20Final_0.pdf. Accessed on 10th Apr 200.

[27] ISTEEBU and ICF International. Institut de Statistiques et d'Études Économiques du Burundi (ISTEEBU), Ministère de la Santé Publique et de la Lutte contre le Sida [Burundi] (MSPLS), and ICF International. 2012. Enquête Démographique et de Santé Burundi 2010. Bujumbura, Burundi: ISTEEBU, MSPLS, and ICF International.

[28] Fink, G., Sudfeld, C.R., Danaei, G., Ezzati, M., Fawzi, W.W. 2014. "Scaling-Up Access to Family Planning May Improve Linear Growth and Child Development in Low and Middle-Income Countries." PLoS ONE 9(7): e102391. Doi: 10.1371/journal.pone.0102391.

[29] IPC. 2017. IPC Acute Malnutrition Analysis. Available at: https://reliefweb.int/sites/reliefweb.int/files/resources/IPC%20AMN%20Burundi%20 communication%20brief%20Sept%20 20 17%20VF%20%28002%29_0.pdf. Accessed on 8th Apr 2020.

[30] CIA.2020. Africa-South Sudan. Found at: https://www.cia.gov/library/publications/the-world-factbook/geos/print_od.html. Accessed on 20th Apr 2020.

[31] USAID. 2020. Food assistance fact sheet-South Sudan. Found at: www.

usaid.gov/south-sudan/food-assistance. Accessed 15th April 2020.

[32] UNOCHA. 2016. South Sudan Food Security Situation, OCHA 5th Jan 2016. Found at: https://www.unocha.org/south-sudan. Accessed on 12th Apr 2020.

[33] UNOCHA. 2017. South Sudan Food Security Snapshot. OCHA, 13 Feb 2017. Found at: https://www.unocha.org/south-sudan https://www.unocha.org/south-sudan.

[34] IPC. 2017. Republic of South Sudan, IPC, 20 Feb 2017. Found at: http://www.ipcinfo.org/fileadmin/user_upload/ipcinfo/docs/IPC_South_Sudan_Key%20Messages_Feb2017.pdf. Accessed on 15th Apr 2020.

[35] IPC. 2017. South Sudan: Acute malnutrition for May 2017 with projections up to July 2017. Found at: ipcinfo.org/ipc-country-analysis/details-map/en/c/1139097/

[36] FAO. 2017. IPC Map of South Sudan, FAO, 6 Nov 2017. Found at: www.fao.org/resilience/mulitimedia/maps/details/en/c//1055744/. Accessed on 10th Apr 2020.

[37] WFP. 2018. Emergency relief operations, WFP 8 Jan 2018. Found at: www.wfp.org/countries/south-sudan. Accessed on 10th March, 2020.

[38] FEWSNET. 2018. East Africa: South Sudan-Catastrophe persists in Akobo and Duk as inter-communal clashes escalate. FEWSNET 22 March 2018. Found at: www.fews.net/east-africa/south-sudan. Accessed on 15th March, 2020.

[39] IPC. 2018. South Sudan: Acute Malnutrition for September with projections up to December 2018. Found at: http://www.ipcinfo.org/ipc-country-analysis/details-map/en/c/1151657/. Accessed on 15th Apr 2020.

[40] IPC. 2019. South Sudan: Acute insecurity and malnutrition situation, Jan 2019 with projections up to July 2019. IPC Jan 2019, Found at: http://www.ipcinfo.org/ipc-country-analysis/details-map/en/c/1151975/. Accessed on 12th Apr 2020.

[41] UNICEF/World Bank. Global data bases/Infant and Young Child Feeding/Joint child malnutrition estimates. WHO Global Health Observatory, 2020. Found at: https://globalnutritionreport.org/resources/nutrition-profiles/africa/eastern-africa/south-sudan/. Accessed on 16th October, 2020.

Chapter 7

Food and Nutrition Security in East Africa (Kenya, Uganda and Tanzania): Status, Challenges and Prospects

Michael N.I. Lokuruka

Abstract

Achieving food and nutrition security remains a tall order for developing countries. The FAO, IFPRI, WFP, UNICEF and other international bodies continue to provide active support in order to achieve global food and nutrition security. However, low technological capability, inefficient production, insignificant economic growth, increasing populations and lately climate variability, affect food production, leading to either stagnation or modest gains in food and nutrition security in different regions of the World. For African countries, food and nutrition security continues to improve, albeit at a slow pace, although the recent breakout of COVID-19 is bound to lead to a decline in food production, in the short and mid-term. In the East African Community, political stability, ambitious economic planning, the quest for higher agricultural productivity, improving educational achievement, improving sanitation and health, are contributing to the improving food and nutrition security. To hasten the process, Kenya, Uganda and Tanzania embraced Vision 2030, Vision 2040 and Vision 2025, respectively. These grand, socio-economic plans bore Vision 2050 in the East African Community and Vision 2063 for the African Union. This chapter examines food and nutrition security in Kenya, Uganda and Tanzania, and provides country-specific recommendations for achieving it. These include investing in agriculture, decelerating population growth, using adaptive research to solve farmer-problems, strengthening farmer-organizations and the formation of cooperatives.

Keywords: East African community, Kenya, Uganda, Tanzania, economic and social development, agriculture, food and nutrition security, status, challenges, prospects

1. Introduction

1.1 Food and nutrition security

The FAO-organized Food Summit in Rome in 1996 recognized the need to ensure physical and economic access to safe and nutritious food, if the nutritional needs of any population have to be met and for them to lead an active and healthy lifestyle [1]. However, the FAO World Food Summit of 2001 refined the definition to include health care and sanitation aspects in the context of the environment in which the food is consumed. Thus food security can be defined in six dimensions that are interrelated, which are: physical availability of food, economic and physical access to food, affordability of the food supply, availability of adequate and safe food, the utilization or the ability of the body to make use of the nutrients and the stability of the dimensions; in summary, the dimensions are access, availability, adequacy, safety, affordability and stability. Even though food is recognized as a universal human right due to its central role in human development, it is currently unmet for billions of people in the world. The state of food and nutrition insecurity is a daily experience in many parts of developing countries, with most countries of Africa being victims of the situation. From the above definition, the United Nations Steering Committee on Nutrition opined that the link of food sufficiency and nutrition status of the consumer should be clearly brought out whenever the subject of food security is discussed. This is because when we consume food, it is supposed to supply the right nutrients in the proportions and form that the body needs for optimal metabolic, physical and physiological functioning. Thus the improved definition that brings out both aspects includes: "access by all people, at all times, by any physical, social and economic means to food that is consumed in adequate quantity and quality, to be able to meet their dietary preferences and needs, and is supported by a sanitary environment, where access to health services and care is assured in order for the consumer to live a healthy and active lifestyle". It therefore follows that any discussion on food and nutrition security, should consider physical access, availability, affordability, adequacy, quality and stability of the food supply. Quality in this respect encompasses not only physical fitness for purpose of the food item, but its being safe and in the form expected for it to be acceptable to the consumer [2]. The food consumed must meet the quality and quantity requirements of age, gender, occupation and health status of the consumer [3]. Adequate and proper nutritional quality of the food supply is an essential prerequisite for maintaining good health status. The critical role nutrition plays in health and human development, warrants greater commitment to the attainment of good nutritional status. The member states of the East African Community (EAC) have ratified a wide range of international covenants and committed themselves to ending hunger and malnutrition among their populations. Building on these commitments, the current article examines the status and prospects for Food and Nutrition Security in the Member States of the East African Community (EAC). It discusses some basic facts of the Region and delves into the subject matter of the thesis, with the situation in Kenya, Uganda and Tanzania, being examined in some detail. The current chapter also provides a set of recommendations for improving the food and nutrition security situation in the future for each country.

1.2 The East African community

The EAC existed as an important trading block up until its break up in 1977 (it was then made up of Kenya, Uganda and Tanganyika-i.e., Tanzania, but without Zanzibar, Pemba and the smaller Islands in the Indian Ocean); It was revived on 30th November 1999, but the instruments for its re-establishment came into effect in 2000. It has a larger country composition, comprising of Kenya, Uganda, Tanzania, Rwanda, Burundi, and South Sudan. On 14th June 2019, the Democratic Republic of the Congo (DRC) requested to join the trading bloc, but the request is yet to be discussed and determined. The region has a current population of over 150 million people, but is likely to surpass 240 million, if the DRC is formally admitted as a member. The EAC as currently constituted is made up of over 200 ethnic groups. The current 6 member states of the EAC appear in **Figure 1**.

Figure 1.
Member states of the EAC (shaded).

1.2.1 Geography of the region

This part of the continent is composed mainly of plateaus, most of the highest elevations on the African continent and the largest lakes in Africa. In Kenya and parts of Tanzania, the highest elevations in the highlands reach as high as 2000–3000 feet above the mean sea level. The twin Rift Valley Systems run across the Region. The Great or Eastern Rift Valley runs from the Red Sea down through Ethiopia and Kenya going downward towards Tanzania, where the faulting activity created Lake Turkana and Tanganyika. The Western Rift System curves around western Uganda and Tanzania and includes Lake Victoria, the largest tropical lake and the largest and second largest fresh water lake in Africa and the World by surface area, respectively. Africa's highest mountain, Mount Kilimanjaro stands on the edge of the Great Rift Valley at above 19,340 feet (5895 metres above sea level) in northeastern Tanzania. Rwanda and Burundi sit on the edge of the western side of the Western Rift System and are a conflagration of hills and valleys that mesh into the fertile tropical forests of the DRC in the west. South Sudan sits between the dry northern Kenya plains, the semi-arid eastern Uganda and western Ethiopia. South Sudan is made up of tropical forests, swamps and grassland. The Imatong Mountains contain South Sudan's highest point, Mount Kinyeti at 10,456 feet above sea level.

1.2.2 Regional weather and vegetation

The climate of the Region is generally tropical, but the high temperatures are tempered by the high elevations, the valleys and hills of Rwanda, Burundi and western Uganda. Precipitation depends on altitude, with western Kenya, South Sudan, most of Uganda, Tanzania, Rwanda and Burundi receiving high amounts of rainfall. Northern Kenya and the Karamoja Region of Uganda, receive low amounts of rainfall ranging from 5 to 40 inches annually, though Karamoja receives slightly hjgher than 40 inches annually. These low rainfall areas have low food production potential and are associated with high poverty indices and therefore poor food and nutrition security. Nomadic pastoralism based on livestock keeping is the major mode of production and livelihood in these semi-arid areas. The region's vegetation is composed of thick woodlands and grassland in the high and wetter elevations, to scanty, thorny shrub and vegetation to desert terrain in the arid and semi-arid plains, respectively. South Sudan is hot with seasonal rainfall as influenced by the annual shift of the Inter-tropical Convergence Zone. Rainfall is heaviest in the southern highlands and reduces towards the north as it merges into the Republic of Sudan.

This chapter examines the economic, food and nutrition security situation in Kenya, Uganda and Tanzania. For each country, some recommendations that are likely to improve food and nutrition security in the long-term are provided.

2. Kenya

2.1 Economy, agriculture and social development

Although the agricultural sector continues to dominate Kenya's economy, only 15–20% of Kenya's total land area has sufficient fertility and rainfall to be farmed, but only 7–8% of the land can be classified as first-class agricultural land. A considerable number of Kenyans make their living off the land, but this trend has continued to decline from the 1980s for various reasons including: rural–urban migration, the low economic gains from the sector, population growth and conversion of agricultural land to residential land, and, sub-division for purposes of inheritance, etc.

Agriculture is the second largest contributor to Kenya's gross domestic product (GDP) after the service sector and fundamentally drives the country's economy, as about 75% of Kenyans earn all or part of their income from the sector. Agriculture generally accounts for 33% of the nation's GDP, but its contribution to the country's GDP has continued to fluctuate over the years as agricultural productivity has either stagnated or declined. This has been observed for major food crops such as wheat and rice. Furthermore, the 15–20% of Kenya's land area that is regarded as suitable for farming is not also utilized efficiently.

Recurrent crises such as drought add to the agriculture-related challenges which largely contribute to the high malnutrition levels in the country. In 2005, agriculture, including forestry and fishing, accounted for 18% of wage employment and 50% of revenue from exports. For decades, the principal cash crops have remained tea, horticultural produce and coffee, with horticultural produce and tea being the major earners of foreign exchange. Horticultural produce and tea accounted for 23% and 22% of total export earnings, respectively. Coffee which has declined in importance due in part to depressed world prices and the decline of land under the crop, accounted for just 5% of export receipts in 2005. The production of major food staples such as maize is subject to sharp weather-related fluctuations. Declines in maize production often times leads to the need for Government to appeal for food aid, as was witnessed in 2004, and even lately in 2016–2017, when as many as 1.8–2.0 million people needed food relief. The expansion of credit to the agricultural sector by the financial sector has enabled farmers to better deal with the large risk of agriculture based on seasonal rainfall and dramatic fluctuations of the prices of agricultural commodities. The expansion of the area under irrigation is another major food policy issue for government as it works to find ways of increasing food production.

Tea, coffee, sisal, pyrethrum, maize, and wheat are grown in the fertile Kenya highlands, which is one of the most successful agricultural production regions in Africa. However, the production of sisal and pyrethrum is declining to levels where there may be no production of these two crops in the near future for various reasons which are outside the realm of the current discussion.

Local livestock breeds (Boran and Zebu) predominate in the semi-arid savanna to the north and east of the country, but exotic dairy breeds such as Friesian, Ayrshire, Sahiwal and crosses of the exotic and local Zebu cattle are kept in the highlands and mid altitudes, with the latter region sustaining the beef breeds. Cash and food crops including coconuts, pineapples, cashew nuts, sugarcane, and maize are grown in most parts of the country.

Kenya Vision 2030, the development blue print for the country, was initiated in 2013 by Emilio Mwai Kibaki, the 3rd President of Kenya. It has the economic, social and political pillars as its anchors; the economic pillar aims at improving the prosperity of all Kenyans through an economic development programme, covering all the regions of Kenya. It aimed to achieve a GDP growth rate of 10% per annum beginning in 2004, but the country has consistently fallen short of the target every subsequent financial year. However, to work towards achieving the target, Kenya is continuing with the tradition of macro-economic stability that has been established since 2002. The New Administration of President Uhuru M. Kenyatta has picked up some key economic deliverables in the Vision, in what in 2018, it has characterized as "The Big Four."

These are:

1. Universal Healthcare,
2. Manufacturing,
3. Affordable Housing and
4. Food Security,

Through the economic pillar and strategy, Kenya aims to build a just and cohesive society with social equity available to all its citizens and enable them live in a clean and secure environment. The vision presents comprehensive social interventions for improving the quality of life of all Kenyans and Kenyan residents. The strategy contains special provisions to help persons living with various disabilities and previously marginalized communities, who may lack a good education, are unemployed and experience poor nutritional status due to high poverty prevalence among them. These policies (and those in the economic pillar) are equally anchored on an all-round strategy of adopting science, technology and innovation (STI) as the implementation tool. The STI concentrates in certain areas for it to contribute to the success of the initiative, including:

- Education and vocational/technical training
- Healthcare
- Water and sanitation
- The environment
- Housing and urbanization

- Gender, youth and vulnerable groups
- Equity and poverty elimination, and,
- National reconciliation, integration and cohesion

2.2 Food and nutrition security

Kenya has a current population of 47.6 million [4] and is generally regarded as water-deficient and food and nutrition insecure. It suffers from frequent droughts and famines with as many as 2–3 million people affected every time a famine or drought occurs, and, about 10 million suffering from chronic food insecurity and poor nutrition. Most of those affected live in the pastoral, semi-arid and arid areas of the country located in the North, Northeast and Northwest of the country, although parts of the Upper Eastern that include the Counties of Kitui, Makueni and Tana River County in the Coastal Region (**Figure 2**), are often also affected. Some of these arid and semi-arid zones receive as little 5–30 inches or more of rain annually. The other category of consumers that is often affected by food and nutrition insecurity is the slum dwellers, who constitute a considerable percentage of the country's population, and, live in the inner cities of the major urban settlements. The Cities of Nairobi, Mombasa, Kisumu, Nakuru and Eldoret hold about 20% of the country's population and will therefore require significant attention in the effort to reduce food and nutrition insecurity in the country. Malnutrition is a public concern and is the single most important contributor to child mortality which stood at 30.6% in every 1000 births by 2018 down from 33.3% in 2015. Malnutrition is mainly due to inadequate food intake and disease, with the underlying factors being poor child care practices, household food insecurity, and inadequate sanitation and health care services, among others. Most of the indicators on food availability, access and affordability, poverty levels and nutritional status are obtained through statistics generated from the Integrated Household Budget Surveys (IHBS) and the Kenya Household and Dietary Surveys (KHDS). The latest IHBS and KHDS were done in 2011 and 2014, respectively. The IHBS surveys show different levels of food poverty across the former eight Kenyan Administrative Provinces, which were abolished after the promulgation of the new Kenya Constitution in 2010 [5].

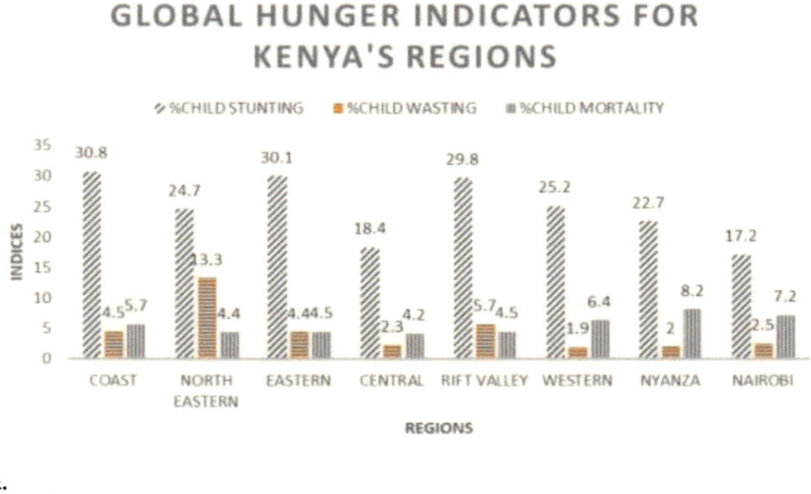

Figure 2.
GHI for Kenya's regions.

They were replaced by 47 Counties, which came into being in March 2013. The IHBS of 2011 showed food poverty levels of 31, 45, 46, 50, 51, 64 and 66% for the then Central, Eastern, Nyanza, Rift Valley, Western, Coast and Northeastern Provinces, respectively. It is likely that the indicators have declined in some of the regions between then and now. Low indicators are normally apparent in the Provinces where nomadic pastoralists are a significant percentage of the population. The pastoralist, semi-arid and arid areas that compose about 70% of the country's land mass and hold about 30% of the human population, are some of the poorest regions of the country, with the worst food poverty, nourishment, health and sanitation indicators. In the counties where nomadic pastoralism dominates as a form of resource use and production, the factors that seem to be major drivers of food and nutrition insecurity include weather anomalies, water scarcity, ethnic resource-based conflicts and displacements, high food prices, depressed livestock sales prices, hardships associated with migration in search of water and pasture for livestock herds by the nomads, cross-border conflicts and livestock pest and disease outbreaks. Climate variability is an ongoing phenomenon that is affecting food production. The rest of the country falls under the agrarian belt, where arable farming is practised. In the agrarian belt, the major drivers for food and nutrition insecurity include poor transport infrastructure, poor market access for farm produce, climate variability, late arrival of government subsidized fertilizer and agro-chemicals, late payments to farmers for crop delivered to depots of the National Cereals and Produce Board, poor management of farmers' cooperatives, depressed food sales prices and crop pests and livestock diseases. Grossly inadequate storage facilities and poor handling and storage practices for cereal grain, pulses and oil seeds, also contribute to food and nutrition insecurity as considerable amounts of produce is lost through microbially-mediated deterioration and pest infestation. Poor purchase prices, delayed payments of deliveries to National Government grain depots, often encourage sales of surplus harvest to middlemen, who despite offering modest prices compared to government agencies have the advantage of on-the-spot cash payments for produce bought. It is envisaged that the provision of storage facilities through the National Cereals and Produce Board, Co-operatives, improvement in road infrastructure, the expansion of rural electrification programmes, adoption of climate-smart agriculture, diversification of the food supply and diets, especially an increase in consumption of fruits and vegetables will lower food and nutrition security indicators and improve consumer nutritional status and health.

The mortality rate of Kenyan children under age five has fallen steadily since 2000 [6], but remains of grave concern. On the positive side, the level of undernourishment among Kenya's children fell in 2001–2003 and again in 2013–2015, but recurring droughts have led to a noticeable rise in levels. A decline was also recently observed after the 2016–2017 drought which affected Kenya and her neighbors, and which resulted in drops in agricultural production, increases in food prices [7, 8], and the consumption of inadequate food of low calorie and protein content. The impact of the current COVID-19 pandemic is expected to be disastrous as agricultural production is expected to fall arising from the lengthy lockdowns and restrictions of movement of goods, people, the imposed curfews and the closing down of businesses.

Kenya's child stunting and child wasting levels have also fallen considerably, with the stunting rate dropping from 35.2–26.0%, and the wasting rate falling from 7.0–4.0% in 2008–2009 and in 2014 [9, 10]. Levels vary substantially between regions and counties, with some having values significantly higher than the national averages. The highest child stunting percentages were found in Kitui County and West Pokot at 45.8% and 45.9%, respectively [10]. Although these Counties have high poverty levels (48 and 57%, respectively, based on national poverty indicators), stunting in Kenya is not perfectly associated with poverty levels. Rather, it seems to be influenced by a complex set of factors that include dietary diversity, feeding and caregiving practices, access to appropriate sanitation and disease prevalence [11, 12]. Wasting is highest in Kenya's northernmost counties: with a value of 22.9% in Turkana, 16.3% in Marsabit, 14.8% in Mandera, 14.3% in West Pokot, and 14.2% in Wajir [10]. These Counties are arid or semi-arid, and are dominated by pastoralism as a form of livelihood and production and therefore have high poverty levels [13, 14]. Moreover, rates of contraception use and women's education levels in these counties are low and fertility rates are high [10]. It has been observed that children's nutritional status is associated with mothers' education and literacy rates [15], both globally and in Kenya, specifically. A study from urban settlements of Nairobi found that maternal education strongly predicts children's nutritional status, when controlling for other socio-economic and demographic factors [16]. Some recent data from Kenya shows that the stunting rate of children whose mothers had no formal education was 31%, while that of children whose mothers had secondary education or higher was 17% [10]. Children's nutrition is also associated with mothers' nutritional status and therefore income. A study from rural Kenya showed a positive correlation between maternal nutrition and children's nutritional status in terms of anthropometric measures [17]. As Kenya attempts to further reduce child undernutrition, albeit with persistent challenges, any gains will be achieved if it addresses infant and young child feeding practices in the Counties. Breastfeeding practices have improved substantially in Kenya, with 61% of children under 6 months exclusively breastfed in 2014, compared with just 32% in 2008–2009 [10, 9]. Meanwhile, in 2014, just 22% of children between 6 and 23 months of age received a minimum acceptable diet [10]. **Figure 2** gives global hunger indicators (GHI) for Kenya's regions.

Although most food and nutrition analyses of Kenya have traditionally focused on rural areas, where rates of child undernutrition tend to be higher than in urban areas, Kenya's population is increasingly urbanizing, and urban food insecurity and undernutrition, are emerging concerns [10, 18, 19]. Urban dwellers are highly vulnerable to food price spikes, which affect their access to affordable food, especially the unemployed, casual labourers who mainly live in the sprawling informal settlements of Nairobi, Kisumu, Nakuru, Mombasa and Eldoret, and increasingly in every major urban centre in the country. Moreover, urban populations live in crowded, poor accommodation, and often lack adequate water, sanitation and therefore live in unhygienic conditions are subject to illness and disease [18, 19]. Child mortality declined much more slowly in urban than in rural areas of Kenya between 1993 and 2008, perhaps because of the deplorable living conditions in urban settlements [20]. In 2014, Nairobi had the second highest child mortality rate among Kenya's regions (**Figure 2**).

Agriculture is considered to have considerable potential to increase household food security and nutrition. Although evidence of the impact of agricultural technologies on relevant outcomes is limited, some studies have shown promising results in Kenya [21]. Dairying and pastoralism play important economic roles among Kenyan smallholder farmers, with significant implications for nutrition. Roughly a quarter of Kenyan households engage in small-scale dairy activities. Studies of pastoralism in four of Kenya's northern, and arid counties–Mandera, Marsabit, Turkana, and Wajir (**Figure 3**) showed that livestock is the main source of livelihood for not less than 57% of households [13, 22]. For pastoralist households, the animals provide the milk consumed by families, and as livestock assets decrease, so does milk consumption affecting children's nutritional status and well-being. Milk consumption at the household level was found to be positively associated with higher body mass index among Samburu youth [23]. Consumption

Figure 3.
The counties of Kenya.

of animal-source foods by Kenyan schoolchildren has also been shown to be positively associated with height and weight gains. A school-feeding programme that tested the effect of different types of snacks given to children found that meat and milk snacks contributed the most to children's arm muscle growth. **Figure 3** shows the current Counties of Kenya.

Kenya is engaged in cash transfer initiatives as a way to lift the poor out of food and nutrition insecurity. The unconditional cash transfer programme for Orphans and Vulnerable Children increased households' food expenditures and dietary diversity, and the consumption of food produced by households themselves. The unconditional cash transfer programme in rural Kenya also increased households' food security and food expenditures, particularly when the transfers are made monthly rather than in a lump sum [24]. Kenya's Hunger Safety Net Programme, an unconditional cash transfer programme, boosted beneficiaries' food consumption relative to controls and increased dietary diversity for poorer households in the project [25, 26].

Nutrition education can also help improve diet quality for children and adults in Kenya. A pilot study in western Kenya showed that providing nutrition education to fathers and grandmothers on proper complementary feeding practices for children raised social support for mothers, and, resulted in the adoption of beneficial child feeding practices [27]. Despite the need to continue addressing malnutrition in the country, micronutrient deficiencies of Vitamin A, Folic acid, Iron, Zinc and Iodine are widespread, with the re-emerging rise in rickets. However, the iodization of salt and fortification of many processed foods, especially the staples with most of the above micronutrients will alleviate the problem. Emerging issues include child obesity, where female children appear more obese and overweight than their male counterparts.

2.3 Prospects

The operationalization of the Food and Nutrition Security Policy of 2011, the placement of access to quality and adequate food access for citizens in the new Kenya Constitution of 2010 [7] as a human right, and support programmes arising thereof, are providing a firm foundation for the country to effectively address the issues of food and nutrition insecurity in a planned and focused manner. This is backed by an increasing number of interventions from the National and the County Governments and International non-Governmental Organizations, with the most notable being the World Food Programe (WFP) and UNICEF, with the focus for the latter being women and children. The Food and Nutrition Policy of 2011 is themed on 3 areas:

a. Optimizing the health of Kenyans through good nutrition

b. Ensuring access and the availability of good quality and affordable food, all the time to consumers

c. Using cost-effective safety nets to protect the vulnerable populations in order to achieve long-term development

The policy broadly recommends providing specific crops for specific agro-climatic zones of the country. With the focus being on the child, one intervention and recommendation from the policy is providing food subsidy and food aid to vulnerable groups and children, in the latter case by strengthening and making school feeding programmes work. The WFP has for many years sustained the school feeding programmes in the semi-arid and arid parts of the country, despite the programme facing logistical as well as policy difficulties. There are other policy instruments that are currently either being finalized or implemented. Major areas of focus that can boost agricultural production and eventually reduce food and nutrition insecurity in Kenya include but are not limited to:

- Enhancing access to agricultural financing: While Kenya represents a vibrant and enabling market for agricultural produce, the enthusiasm by the banking sector to service commercial agriculture is lacking, as only about 4% of commercial bank lending is for agribusiness, despite most Kenyans being employed in agriculture or agriculture-related businesses.

- Increasing the use of fertilizer: Fertilizer use remains inadequate in Kenya as the Government's fertilizer subsidy programme is inefficient, and often disproportionately benefits more medium/large scale famers than small-scale farmers. Small-scale farmers are the backbone of the country's agriculture sector. Making the scheme work for small-scale farmers and ensuring that it is efficient, transparent, and targets them, has the potential of raising agricultural output and productivity.

- Establishing private sector-led commodity trading: Similar to the situation in most Africa countries, the Kenya government retains a big role in marketing agricultural outputs, especially maize, the staple cereal crop for a majority of the country's population, thereby leaving little room for private sector participation. Further, the National Cereals and Produce Board buys maize at a premium above the price determined by market forces. These interventions edge out private sector players somewhat, resulting in reduced availability of public finance for other potentially more useful expenditures, e.g., extension services and farmer training.

- Investing in irrigation: While over 80% of Kenya's land area is arid and semi-arid, 2% of the arable land is under irrigation compared to an average of 6% in Sub-Saharan Africa and 37% in Asia [28]. The low usage of irrigation means Kenya's agriculture is fully rain-dependent and susceptible to shocks due to droughts. Investing in irrigation and water management for farmers, can reduce productivity shocks and raise the sector's total productivity, potentially improving food and nutrition security in the country.

- Supporting stronger farmer organizations: Kenya has many geographically dispersed smallholders who are not integrated into key agriculture value chains. Dispersion increases production costs and reduces small-scale farmers' competitiveness. It is envisaged that building stronger farmer-organizations fosters economic inclusion of smallholders and increase their market power, thereby raising their incomes and productivity. Further, while value addition to agricultural commodities remains low in the country, increasing the value addition of agricultural commodities can create more jobs and reduce poverty. A set of recommendations that mirrors the above discussion is provided below.

In conclusion, a decade of rapid economic growth from 2003 to 2013, the inclusion of food and nutrition security in the government's 'big four' priorities in 2018, constitutional changes that devolved administrative responsibilities to county governments since 2013, and the country's openness to innovation, offer **opportunities for the achievement of SDG 2** on Zero Hunger and improved nutrition in Kenya. However, even though the country has recently acquired lower-middle-income status, the **increased wealth has not benefited all Kenyans equally.** Over **one third of the population still lives under the international poverty line** (of $1.25/day) and **socio-economic disparities between regions and ethnic groups remain. Access to adequate quantities of nutritious food remains a challenge for many**, especially in the arid and semi-arid regions, which make up over 80% of the country's land area. Rapid population growth, at 2.9% annually, climate change, stagnating agricultural production and inefficient food value chains are additional challenges. Food insecure families typically live in rural areas, are poor and depend on daily agricultural labour for income. **Families headed by women are more likely to be food insecure than those headed by men. Some recommendations to address some of the above concerns follow.**

2.4 Recommendations

- The National and County Governments should minimize climate variability effects on the agriculture sector by expanding viable irrigation schemes, emphasizing the adoption of drought tolerant crops including cassava, sorghum, millet, potatoes and the adoption of small dairy stock by households. These animals are potential sources of income and high biological value protein in the form of meat and milk

- The country should continue scaling up programmes for treatment of malnutrition among vulnerable groups as well as implementing common public health measures such as vaccination, deworming, supplementation and water and sanitation in pastoralist counties, where livestock keeping is a major economic activity

- Prioritize policies and programmes that increase farm and crop productivity, food and nutrition security, and resilience of small-scale farmers and pastoralists. Such steps will be increasingly vital for Kenya's future food and nutrition security improvement as the percentage of the population that is dependent on nomadic pastoralism and rain-fed agriculture is large and highly vulnerable to climate change and droughts

- Continue promoting education for women and girls, particularly in areas dominated by pastoralism that are characterized by low female education attainment rates and high child wasting scores. Women's education and child nutrition have been shown to be positively linked

- Strengthen support for improvements in the WASH environment in Kenya, including implementation of the provisions of the Kenya Environmental Sanitation and Hygiene Policy, 2016–2030. Urban settlements, rural areas, and informal settlements have the lowest levels of improved sanitation, sometimes lacking it completely, compared with planned urban areas [29]. Inadequate WASH facilities and practices are detrimental to human health and nutrition, especially for children

- Strengthen political and educational support to the production, distribution, and consumption of nutritious crops such as vitamin A-rich orange-fleshed sweet potatoes and green and yellow leafy vegetables, and ensure that low income households have access to these products, either by way of them being subsidized or as food aid, where the households are extremely poor, single, and living with disabilities and/or are unemployed

- Ensure that food security and good nutrition are given priority at the national and county levels, recognizing the vital role that County Governments must play given Kenya's devolved government structure. Food and nutrition security decisions should be guided by the data that exists at the county level.

- The Food Security Bill, 2017, and the National Nutrition Action Plan, 2018–2022, are largely still under consideration for implementation [30, 31]. Their implementation would ensure that food and nutrition security is prioritized in Kenya

- Enforce the provisions of "The Breastfeeding Mothers Bil"l (2017), which aims to protect women's right to breastfeed in the workplace and public places. This bill once enforced should further promote breastfeeding in Kenya, which is critical to infant health and development

- Strengthen community capacity to prepare for future nutrition crises by providing staffing, training, and resources for community-based management of acute malnutrition

- Support innovative programmes that provide the support of the integrated management of acute malnutrition, with contributions from local and international partners to deter food and nutrition insecurity

3. Uganda

3.1 The economy, agriculture and social development

Uganda's economy has in recent years grown at a slower pace, thus reducing its impact on incomes and poverty reduction. Average annual growth rate was 4.5% from 2011 to 2016, compared to the 7% achieved during the 1990s and early 2000s [32]. The slowdown was mainly driven by adverse weather, unrest in South Sudan, private sector credit constraints, and the poor management of public sector projects. However, the economy rebounded in the second half of 2017, driven largely by growth in information and communication technology services and favorable weather conditions for the agricultural sector. GDP growth adjusted for inflation was above 5% in 2018 and rose further to about 6% in 2019 [33]. For better performance, the outlook would require continued good weather, favorable external conditions to boost demand for exports and an increase in foreign direct investment (FDI) and inflows as oil production draws closer, and capital investments are executed as planned. Reliance on rain-fed agriculture, however, remains a downside risk to growth, personal incomes and export earnings from the agriculture sector.

In the long-run, delays and poor management of public investment programs could prevent the productivity gains expected from enhanced infrastructure, while acceleration in domestic arrears may have an adverse impact on private investment which may further limit the extension of credit. Finally, regional instability and a continued influx of refugees is likely to undermine exports and disrupt growth in refugee hosting parts of Uganda. The intensifying conflicts in South Sudan and the Democratic Republic of Congo, currently Uganda's 2nd and 4th top export destinations, respectively, is likely to negatively affect the growth of Uganda's exports.

Uganda has a population of close to 42 million by 2019 estimates [34] and has an equatorial type of climate with rainfall in most of the country standing annually at 1000 to 1500 mL, but which can be as high as 2000 mL in the Lake Victoria basin [35]. Karamoja Region, parts of Teso and Acholi Regions in the north, receive much less rainfall with a tendency to be unpredictable and unreliable. The Official Government report issued in 2014 showed that about 83% of the Ugandan population can be classified under Phase 1 Category of minimal or no food insecurity threats, and, was able to meet their dietary and non-food requirements without stress [36]. The report showed wide access and affordability of the food available in the markets with the majority of the population being able to obtain three meals a day of a diversified diet. Only about 1% of the general Ugandan population qualified to be in IPC category 3-a situation of food crisis. Uganda like other EAC member states faces similar food insecurity threats such as livestock and crop diseases. The common crop diseases include: banana bacterial wilt, cassava brown streak disease, stalk borer disease and recently, maize necrosis which was first spotted in Kenya. Regional cooperation would be required to find solutions to most of these economic and food security threats. In the livestock sector, Food and Mouth Disease often breaks out, as well as a number of other common livestock diseases that affect the livestock trade across the EAC trading bloc. They are a constant hindrance to planned improvements to food security in the livestock sub-sector.

3.1.1 Political context and development challenges

After the end of the armed conflict in 1986, the Government formed by the National Resistance Movement introduced a host of structural reforms and investments, most of which led to the long and sustained period of high growth and poverty reduction between 1987 and 2010. Policy and legal frameworks continue to improve, notably through the operationalization of the Public Financial Management Act, 2015 [37], though gaps in implementation in procurement and anti-corruption remain major concerns, with consequences for development indicators and directly for public sector-led enablers of food availability and access.

Uganda surpassed the *Millennium Development Goals* target of halving poverty by 2015, and made significant progress in reducing the proportion of the population that suffers from hunger, and in promoting gender equity and economically empowering women. According to the Uganda Poverty Assessment of 2013, more

Figure 4.
Regions of Uganda (note that Teso, Acholi and Karamoja are in eastern and northern regions, respectively).

than 67% of the population lived above the extreme poverty line of US $1.90/day. However, the vulnerability for every 2–3 Ugandans falling back into poverty exists. Estimates from the Uganda National Household Survey of 2016/2017 suggest that the proportion of the population living below the national poverty line rose slightly from 20% in financial year (FY) 2012/2013 to about 21% in FY 2016/2017 [38]. All Uganda's regions registered an increase in the number of poor persons with the notable exception of Northern Region (**Figure 4**), which is the poorest, and where poverty, decreased from 44 to 33%. With one-third of children under five being stunted, Uganda is among the 20 countries worldwide with the highest prevalence of under-nutrition. Stunting in rural compared to urban areas stands at 36% and 19%, respectively. At over 3%, Uganda's annual population growth rate is among the highest in the world, despite observed reduction in fertility rate. Uganda's population of 42 million is expected to reach 100 million by 2050, while the annual urban growth rate of 5.2% is among the highest in the world and is expected to grow from 6.4 million (2014) to 22 million by 2040 [39]. Uganda's refugee population has almost tripled since July 2016 and was around 1.8 million by the end of 2019, making it the largest refugee host in Africa, and the third largest in the world. While its open-door refugee policy is one of the most progressive in the world, as refugees enjoy access to social services, land and can move and work freely, the continued influx is straining host community-refugee relations, service delivery and is likely to negatively influence environmental sustainability.

3.2 Food and nutrition security

Despite producing a variety of food crops and animal food products, malnutrition remains a problem and therefore pockets of under-nourishment and hunger co-exist. Micronutrient deficiencies are common and are exhibited as goiter, vitamin A deficiency and iron-deficiency anemia in the general population, though more common in the poor, children and women of child-bearing age. High malnutrition and under-nutrition rates are generally due to predisposing diseases, HIV/AIDS, inadequate food intake, ignorance, cultural taboos, poverty, etc. The Uganda Food and Nutrition Policy of 2003 emphasized the promotion of good nutritional status of Ugandans through multi-sectoral and coordinated interventions that focused on food security, improved nutrition and increased incomes [40]. The country conducts periodic national income and expenditure surveys, with the latest being the 2009/2010 Uganda National Household Survey. The survey estimated that the incidence of income poverty in Uganda fell by 6.6% points in the 2005/2006 financial year from 31.1 to 24.5% in 2010 [41]. The incidence of income poverty in rural and urban areas was estimated at 27.2 and 9.1, respectively [41].

Although Uganda currently produces sufficient food to meet the needs of its growing population, the absolute number of Ugandans unable to access recommended calories still remains significant in all regions due to the uneven distribution of food, access constraints related to seasonality factors, poverty, inequality in regional wealth distribution and the burden of diseases. The proportion of the population unable to access adequate calories decreased nationally from 23% in 1997 to 15% in 2006 [40]. However, the persistent high rates of malnutrition in children under 5 are symptomatic of the underlying problems of inadequate access to food, suboptimal infant feeding practices, poor health care and sanitation and hygiene practices within the different regions of the Country. It is estimated that more than 30–38% of children suffer from chronic malnutrition (stunting), while about 15% are underweight and 6% suffer from acute malnutrition [42]. Malnutrition in all its forms remains largely a "hidden problem" since a majority of children affected are moderately malnourished and identifying malnutrition in these children without regular assessments is difficult [42]. Increasingly, Uganda similar to other developing countries is experiencing the double burden of malnutrition where high levels of under-nutrition co-exist with a growing prevalence of overweight and obesity. Malnutrition plays a major role in child morbidity and mortality as wasting and underweight have been shown to significantly increase the risk of both morbidity and mortality in children [42]. Vitamin A and iron deficiencies also carry an increased risk of morbidity and mortality in children [43]. Vitamin A deficiency seems to be linked with an increased risk of mortality from measles and severe diarrhoeal diseases [43], while iron deficiency carries significant adverse consequences for child development [44]. Malnutrition starts early in infancy for children in Uganda. The substantial proportion of children born with low birth weight suggests that high fertility rates, short birth intervals, young maternal age and maternal malnutrition are likely factors that contribute significantly and adversely to child malnutrition from birth. High childhood disease infection rates may be attributable to poor feeding practices, where liquids other than breast milk might be introduced early, such that these foods, if not sanitary enough and safe to eat, serve as avenues for disease spread. As the prevalence of stunting increases with age in children, it is a reflection of continuous nutritional deprivation of children from an early age and as they grow. The prevalence of stunting is highest in northern and southwest Uganda, although the rate of decline since 2001 is fastest in the western region and slowest in the northern and eastern regions. The prevalence of underweight is highest in the East, Central, Northern and Southwest regions, and the rate of decline is slower than the rate of change for stunting. Wasting is rising in all regions, with the smallest increase in Central Region [42]. In women, chronic energy deficiency was 12% in the 2006 Uganda Demographic and Health Survey and has been rising across all regions [42]. Overweight and obesity in women is also rising, but most rapidly in urban areas, Western and Central Regions [42]. Deficiencies in Vitamin A and Iodine, and Iron-deficiency anemia (IDA) remain significantly prevalent as discussed earlier. Vitamin A deficiency affects 20% of women and children, and IDA affects 73% of preschool children and 49% of women of child-bearing age [42]. The immediate causes of malnutrition for children in Uganda continue to be the high disease burden resulting from malaria, diarrhoeal diseases and acute respiratory infections, as well as inadequate dietary intake resulting from suboptimal infant feeding practices, as is commonly found in other developing economies. While breastfeeding is nearly universal, exclusive breastfeeding tapers off rapidly and by six months, only 11% of infants are exclusively breastfed. In addition, late initiation of breastfeeding (86%) and the use of pre-lacteal feeds (54%) are common [42]. Early introduction of foods and liquids and inappropriate complementary feeding are also widespread. Adequate feeding practices are used for only 28% of children under two, when considering continued breastfeeding, appropriate frequency of feeding and diet diversity, three key indicators of adequate complementary feeding. Infant and young child feeding (IYCF) practices are suboptimal, and while social and behavior change communication (SBCC) is one response to address this, SBCC alone will not adequately improve feeding practices. Poverty and food insecurity at the household level play a significant role, but women's lack of control over their time, their competing household and reproductive roles may undermine their IYCF capabilities. To succeed, SBCC efforts must engage men as partners in change. The underlying causes of malnutrition in Uganda remain inadequate water and sanitation, lack of dietary diversity, inadequate health infrastructure and access to health care and food insecurity [42]. Although access to health services has improved in the past decade, the quality of the services has remained generally poor [42]. From casual observations by this author on a recent trip to Uganda (December, 2019), sanitation and hygiene has not improved, if not worsened in marginalized areas like Karamoja and northern Uganda, and is exacerbated by increasing urbanization and population rise. Food insecurity varies regionally, with the Northern Region suffering from the highest levels of food insecurity, followed by parts of East and East Central Regions and parts of Southwest Uganda. Common causes of food insecurity across Uganda are the lack of diversification in livelihoods, high dependence on agriculture and wage labour, declining wages and rising food prices. While poverty declined across Uganda from 56% in 1992 to 31% in 2006 [42], improvements in the prevalence of poverty are largely attributable to economic growth rather than income distribution and welfare improvement. In fact, income inequality between the wealthy and the poor has steadily widened. Gender inequality seems to be significantly intertwined with poverty and food insecurity in Uganda and has been identified as a primary reason for the persistent poverty. Poverty may be gendered as income inequality seems to be rising as a high percentage of women lack access to resources such as capital. Gender inequality may therefore exacerbate food insecurity for women and children. While 80% of women contribute labour for food production, they own less than 8% of the land on which to farm [42]. Men may earn significantly more than women but spend more of their income on non-food items, while women are left to close the household food security gap. Women are the primary caregivers in families, but may have the least decision-making power; as a result, they have less control over their family care role and time, than they should. In Uganda, women's low involvement and high fertility rates are two critical factors that undermine health and nutrition outcomes in their children. Taking the multiplicity of factors into account, gender inequality substantially undermines women's capabilities to achieve and ensure food security for their families. This situation calls for approaches that improve the design and delivery of nutrition services to prevent, reduce and control malnutrition at the policy, leadership and programme levels, as well as to promote coordination and resource mobilization. Despite the above gloomy picture, Uganda's nutrition situation is better than many other countries in eastern and southern Africa, as Uganda currently produces sufficient food to meet the needs of most of its growing population. Nationally, the proportion of the population unable to access adequate calories decreased from 15% in 2006 to 11% in 2015 [45], and the country is likely to meet the SDG 2 with robust policies in place. **Figure 4** presents a Map of Uganda showing the regions of the country.

3.3 Prospects

Due to the increasing population and deforestation of the country, more arable land is being brought under cultivation for more food production. However, the continuing influx of refugees from South Sudan due to the civil war in that country, political instability further north in the Republic of Sudan and a host of internal factors, are likely to impact negatively on the country's food production capacity. Although indicators of food poverty, malnutrition and under-nutrition are yet to rise significantly, the increasing population and depressed economic growth are likely to negatively affect the food security and nutrition status in the country in the long-term. Rainfall in 2019 remained erratic in most of Uganda as influenced by Cyclone Idai that affected much of southern Africa, and whose effects spilled into parts of Central and Eastern Africa. The effects of this and other natural factors are largely unpredictable, but the outlook does not seem beyond redemption as Uganda can largely feed its people. Recent trade deals with Kenya and the opening of the Kenya-Uganda border with the aim of minimizing interruptions in trade and travel, is already increasing food trade between Uganda's border Counties and Kenya's

Counties of Trans Nzoia, Bungoma, Busia, Kakamega and Turkana. Uganda is the net gainer from these commercial transactions, and its economy is bound to benefit from the increased trade and the likely increased local agricultural output to meet the increasing demand for more food in Kenya. The analysis of the food and nutrition outlook in Uganda indicates that:

- Nutrition indicators are generally improving, but the rate of change is slow
- Under-nutrition which coexists with over-nutrition is increasing
- Food and nutrition security is being undermined by large family sizes,
- Changing gender roles are affecting food and nutrition security in families
- Poor health infrastructure is undermining nutrition outcomes
- Income and wealth disparities are increasing between regions, classes and genders

In conclusion, 89% of Uganda's population is food secure. This population still has normal access to food from their own production and in the market. Food prices in the markets are affordable, and consumers can experience an acceptable food consumption score as most can afford at least three meals per day of a diversified diet. They also have adequate energy intake. Eleven percent of the total population in the country is chronically food insecure. These are scattered in the Karamoja, Teso and Acholi districts and in the slums in the major cities of Kampala and Entebbe. The food security prospects for Karamoja are expected to remain volatile and unpredictable. Food availability is not a limiting factor in most regions of Uganda except in Karamoja, East, Central and West Nile, where production and productivity, frequent dry spells and lack of extension services constrain food production. Although food is largely available, food access and utilization are major limiting factors in the three regions but minor limiting factors in other regions. This has been attributed to the low level of incomes, poor storage practices, lack of awareness of what constitutes good nutrition, cultural food preferences, poor sanitary and food preparation practices and wastage of food during harvest periods due to festivities.

3.4 Recommendations

The semi-aridity of Karamoja, parts of Teso and Acholi Regions, the inevitability of negative effects of climate variability on food production and the increasing food demand by the increasing country's population means that, there is urgent need to put in place different strategies to secure food for all Ugandans. Some workable recommendations include:

- Establishing programmes and mechanisms for slowing down population growth
- Developing a comprehensive national system based on enabling enhanced and sustainable, efficient food production through the use of modern technologies throughout Uganda's arable regions. The new technologies should be research and innovation-driven

- The formation of collaborative partnerships that diversify food sources, as well as implementing legislation and policies that are geared to improving nutrition, while reducing food waste

- Developing a national agriculture strategy that encourages the production of crops well suited to the various local environments and promotes a production strategy that builds on the country's comparative advantages

- More efficient use of the available arable land for food production and semi-arid lands for better livestock farming systems.

- Reducing the rate of deforestation as it impacts negatively on food production, food security and therefore economic growth. Re-afforestation is recommended to replenish the declining forest cover

- Creating a well-planned international trade and investment strategy, that can help hedge against volatility and food shortages, while spurring economic growth. Creating trading and processing hubs should help the country gain access to food supplies whenever necessary, either internally or through imports

- Planning for efficient domestic markets, and transport systems that emphasize reduction of food waste and curbing shortages

- The formation of cooperatives which can make it easier for farmers and other entrepreneurs to obtain credit

- Creating strategic reserves of food and water to take care of year-to-year variations in rainfall and food output, as well as any man-made disruptions in food supply across the country and those due to the vagaries of nature

- Reducing the influence of gender inequality on food security for women and children, by empowering more women and women more

4. United REPUBLIC of Tanzania

4.1 The economy and social development

With a population of 55–56 million people (2016 estimates), Tanzania has had a good economic growth run over the last decade averaginga 6–7% annually [46]. Although the absolute poverty index for the country decreased, the number of those living in abject poverty has not reduced noticeably due to the high popula-t2ion growth rate. Depending on weather patterns, the country can be split into two main climatic zones-the drought prone bimodal rainfall zone, situated mainly in the north and west of the country and the Unimodal zone in the south and east of the country [46]. In the bimodal rainfall zones, vulnerability to food insecurity is caused by such factors as water shortages, high food prices and the effects of drought on households. Levels of food poverty and malnutrition are higher in these areas than in the unimodal rainfall areas.

Tanzania ranked 152 out of 187 countries in the 2011 UN Human Development Index and number 54 out of 79 on the 2012 Global Hunger Index. While Tanzania has been a low-income country (though it has from early 2020 ascended to low-mid-income status) for quite long, it has experienced relatively stable economic growth in recent years, accelerating from 3.5% in the 1990s to approximately 7% in the 2000s. Effective fiscal and monetary policies largely insulated the country from recent international shocks; the maintenance of such policies, as well as investment in infrastructure and high profit yielding businesses are needed for such growth to continue [47]. Despite its economic growth, poverty remains prevalent in the country, particularly in rural areas, similar to any developing country. Approximately 30 million people, or 75 percent of the population, live in rural areas, with the rural households making up 80% of the country's poor [47]. Agriculture accounts for 45% of Tanzania's GDP and provides livelihoods for up to 80% of the country's population [48]. While Tanzania's food self-sufficiency has ranged from 88 to 112% over the past 8 years, localized food deficits are rampant. The low agricultural productivity makes it difficult to achieve significant strides towards poverty reduction and food security. Tanzania's agriculture is characterized by low adoption of new and functional technologies, limited infrastructure and high transportation costs, a lack of adequate market access, and high rates of taxation and non-tariff trade barriers. The Government has made recent commitments to agricultural reform and improvement, such as the "Agriculture First Program", and considerable budgetary allocation to agriculture. Similarly, agribusiness development is being encouraged under such programmes as the "Southern Agricultural Growth Corridor of Tanzania". Tanzania has some of the highest levels of malnutrition among African countries. Approximately 42% of children under five suffer from malnutrition and stunting [48]. Despite sustained and steady growth, over the past two decades, and the achievement of significant progress in economic, social and human development, the resultant progress has not benefited all sectors of society and inequality has widened.

The country currently produces enough food to feed its population, but the poorest and most marginalized families–including refugees have limited access to it. The agricultural sector is largely dominated by smallholder farmers but production is stagnant, while the population is expected to double by 2050. The effects of climate change are deepening the vulnerability of agriculture to disasters. Households in the bimodal rainfall zone feel steep food prices which on comparison can be as high as 60% higher than those felt by families in the unimodal zones of the country. Economic growth for the country has been on the upsurge for most of the 2000–2010 decade [49], though the improvement in food and nutrition security has not proportionately benefitted from the economic growth experienced in the decade. The Tanzania National Bureau of Statistics reports that real GDP growth was 7.0% in 2018, slightly higher than the 6.8% in 2017.

Zanzibar and Pemba Islands have a population of about 1.3 million people with an estimated annual growth rate of 2.8% (estimates for 2016). Of this number, an estimated 14% may fall into the severely food insecure IPC Phase 3-Crisis level or at worst into the Phase 4-Emergency situation and require immediate food assistance in the dry season which comes normally between July and September [50). This may happen when below normal rains fall in the previous year. This number is normally expected to decrease slightly to about 12% of the population in the October to December period [50]. The most food insecure districts are Kaskazini A, Micheweni and Magharibi. Of main concern is the population in IPC Phase 4 (Emergency) in Kaskazini A and Micheweni in the October to December period. This requires urgent action to protect livelihoods, reduce gaps in food requirement in order to reduce the potential for acute malnutrition in the group. The majority of the population (69%) mainly live in IPC Phase 2 (stressed) and is only able to afford minimally adequate food consumption, but are unable to afford essential non-food expenditures without engaging in irreversible coping strategies [50]. Households who would be most affected are those who depend on agriculture in both Unguja and Pemba. The main driver of food insecurity is reduced harvest caused by poor Vuli rainfall in October to December and a prolonged dry season that would be experienced in January to March or heavy rainfall experienced towards the end of Masika (resulting in flooding and water logging of soils). These weather shocks often lead to shocks in livelihoods and acute food insecurity, especially for poor households particularly in Micheweni. Shortage of Vuli rainfall significantly affects food availability in farming households. The Vuli season is the most important season for food security in Zanzibar as most of the annual crops are planted in the season. The outcome of poor performance of Vuli rains lowers production below normal production levels, leading to low production of cassava, sweet potatoes, fruits and vegetables. These crops are not only important for household food security, but are also the main source of income for households who depend on the sale of these food crops to meet other basic family needs.

Despite any significant reduction in crop production, food availability at national level is not an issue given the opportunity Zanzibar has of importing food commodities from Mainland Tanzania. The biggest problem is, however, the price of these commodities that usually goes up significantly. Food prices in Zanzibar are always on an increasing trend, resulting in reduced household purchasing power and consequently affecting access to adequate and nutritious food. Although in the Micheweni and Kaskazini A Districts there are numbers of people who may not afford enough food, their situation will normally improve as these areas will be in the Clove harvesting season from October to December. Usually during this season, opportunities for income generation rise as short term jobs abound along the clove picking value chain. However, to avert the situation, it is recommended that the Government and implementing partners support the affected communities by provide farming inputs during the subsequent planting season.

It is envisioned that through Vision 2025, Tanzania agriculture will be transformed from a low productivity industry to a modern and semi-industrialized one that is supported by integrated services that would be available equally in the urban and rural areas [51].

4.2 Agriculture, food and nutrition security

Agriculture generates 30% of the country's export earnings [52]. Approximately 46% of Tanzania's total land mass is suitable for agricultural production, and the country can be a net exporter of food, if appropriate and functional food production strategies are put in place. However, only part of this arable land is marginally suitable for food production due to such factors as infertile soils, soil erosion, land degradation, and droughts. Moreover, 25% of the land is under wildlife reserves and protected forests. The country also has over 23% of its land mass being suitable for irrigated agriculture, thus demonstrating the potential for higher food security, if the land was put to such use. The country has a self-sufficiency ratio of 123 for maize, implying surplus production in this staple crop. Livestock keeping is the most important agricultural activity in most parts of the country, including the marginally-endowed agricultural areas and engages about 36% of households. The share of the livestock sector to the GDP was more than 7% in 2015, while its contribution was more than 30% to the agriculture-related contribution of the GDP in the same period [53]. Generally, the self-sufficiency ratio for food for the country between 2012/2013 and 2015/2016 FY has been over 100%, but variations exist at regional, district and household levels. According to the Tanzania Household Nutrition Survey of 2015–2016,the rate of stunting in children under the age of 5 years was 35% (reflecting cumulative effects of acute malnutrition), with 5% of children being wasted (too thin for their age), while 4% are overweight and 14% being under-weight [54]. The mixed news is that the extent of stunting and underweight in children declined over the period 1999–2016, but wasting remained unchanged over the same period. Paradoxically for unexplained reasons, all the three nutritional/health indicators are highest in children in the major food production areas of the southern and southwestern highlands, an observation that requires addressing. They are lowest in children in the highest wealth quartile, but are highest in children in the lowest wealth quartile.

4.3 Prospects

Despite efforts between 2007 and 2016 that have reduced the country's poverty rate from 34.4% to 26.8%, the absolute number of poor people has held at about 13 million (approximately 27–28% of the population) [55] partly due to the high population growth rate. Based on the Household Budget Survey of 2017/18, it seems likely that the downward trend in the poverty rate will continue despite it becoming gradual. Government efforts to expand access to social services like education, health, and water have been undermined by their declining quality. This implies that the slowing of factors that contribute most to improved GHI, and any gains in food and nutrition security in the short-term, will therefore be gradual. Real GDP growth is projected to remain in the range of 5–6% over the medium term. This outlook will depend on favorable weather conditions, the steady implementation of reforms to improve the business environment, good fiscal management, and the ability of the Government to address vulnerabilities in the financial sector. The maintenance of low inflation will be underpinned by favorable food supplies and stable global energy prices. The COVID-19 breakout may, however, complicate matters for the country's economy and food security as expected of other Countries of the EAC Region, though the fact that the country did not go into lockdown may mean that it comes off better than its neighbors.

4.4 Recommendations

- As agricultural productivity remains low and poses a significant challenge to poverty reduction and food security, Government should endeavor to remove challenges related to low adoption of new technologies and improve infrastructure in order to reduce transportation costs and market access

- Government should effect medium and long term interventions to reduce the wasting trends of children in the southern and southwestern highlands, which are also the best agriculturally-endowed regions of the country

- It is critical for the country to arrest the observed overweight trends in children through school education and more physical activities, while simultaneously executing parental education

- The Ministry of Agriculture should embark on irrigated agriculture in marginal areas by the use of appropriate and research-driven investments and technologies

- The Food industry should explore the potential for value addition of crop and livestock sector production for export to the EAC and other regional food-deficient countries

- Government requires to manage population growth so that it is in tandem with food production and services provision
- The Government of Tanzania and Development Partners require to take care of any food short falls that may be experienced in Zanzibar and Pemba islands due to short rains in the Vuli season during which period families face food shortages and are therefore likely to experience IPC 2–3 classification of food and nutrition insecurity.
- Support the affected communities by provide farming inputs during the subsequent planting seasons
- Improve the under-execution of public development projects, and,
- Create policies that raise FDI inflows and improved private sector credit growth
- Ensure that any economic growth benefits all sectors of society and social inequality is reduced

Acronyms

EAC	East African Community
FAO	Food and Agriculture Organization of the United Nations
FDI	Foreign Direct Investment
FY	financial year
GDP	gross domestic product
GHI	global hunger indicators
GoK	Government of Kenya
GoU	Government of Uganda
IFPRI	International Food Policy Research Institute
IPC	Integrated Food Security Phase Classification
SDGs	sustainable development goals
UN	United Nations
UNICEF	United Nations Children's Fund
WFP	World Food Programme
WASH	water, sanitation and hygiene

Author details

Michael N.I. Lokuruka
Department of Food Science, Nutrition and Technology, Karatina University,Box 1957-10101, Karatina, Kenya

*Address all correspondence to: mlokuruka@gmail.com; mlokuruka@karu.ac.ke

References

[1] Birgit Niclasen, Michal Molcho, Steven Arnfjord, and Christina Schnohr. Conceptualizing and contextualizing food insecurity among Greenland children. Int. J. Circumpolar health. Vol. 72, DOI. 10.3402/ijch.v72i0.19928. First published online on May 16th 2013.

[2] Lokuruka, MNI. 2002. Quality and Food Safety Assurance in the Fish Industry. Amu Press, Nakuru, Kenya

[3] Davidson R., Passmore R and Eastwood, MA. 1986. Davidson and Passmore Human Nutrition and Dietetics. Churchill Livingstone, Edinburgh.

[4] Kenya National Bureau of Statistics (KNBS). 2019. Kenya Population Census, 2019, National Treasury and Ministry of Planning, KNBS, Nairobi.

[5] Government of Kenya. 2010. Constitution of Kenya, 2010, Office of the Attorney-General, Nairobi.

[6] UN IGME. 2019. Levels and Trends in child mortality, UNICEF, 2019, New York.

[7] WFP. 2017a. Famine early warning systems network (FEWS NET) 2017a. Kenya Food Security Outlook, WFP Country Office, Nairobi.

[8] WFP. 2017b. FEWS NET 2017b. Kenya Food Security Outlook, WFP Country Office, Nairobi.

[9] KNBS and ICF Macro 2010. Kenya Demographic and Health Survey 2008-2009. Calverton, Maryland. KNBS and ICF Macro.

[10] Kenya National Bureau of Statistics, Ministry of Health, National AIDS Control Council, Kenya Medical Research Institute, National Council for Population and Development and ICF International. 2015. Kenya Demographic and Health Survey 2014. Nairobi, Kenya and Rockville, MD: KNBS and The DHS Program/ICF International.

[11] KNBS. 2018. Kenya Demographic and Health Survey 2008-09. Calverton, Maryland: KNBS and ICF Macro.

[12] Eberwein, Julia Dayton; Kakietek, Jakub Jan; De Beni, Davide; Moloney, Grainne; Pereira, Audrey Leslie; Akuoku, Jonathan Kweku; Volege, Marjorie; Matu, Sicily; Shekar, Meera. 2016. An investment framework for nutrition in Kenya: reducing stunting and other forms of child malnutrition. Health, nutrition, and population discussion paper. ashington, D.C. World Bank Group. Found at: https://www.documents.worldbank.org/curated/en/437531489040369631/An-investment-framework-for-nutrition-in-Kenya-reducing-stunting-and-other-forms-of-child-malnutrition.

[13] Krätli S and Swift J. 2014. Counting pastoralists in Kenya-determining the magnitude of the pastoralist sector in Kenya. DLCI/REGLAP Report, Nairobi.

[14] KNBS and SID, 2013. Pulling apart or pooling together-exploring inequalities in Kenya. KNBS (Kenya National Bureau of Statistics) and SID (Society for International Development), Nairobi.

[15] Ruel MT, Alderman H and the Maternal and Child Nutrition Study Group. Nutrition- sensitive interventions and programmes: how can they help to accelerate progress in improving maternal and child nutrition? The Lancet 382, p 536.

[16] Abuya BA, J Ciera, and Kimani-Murage. 2012. Effect of mother's education on child's nutritional status in the slums of Nairobi. BMC Pediatrics **12(1):80, June 2012.**

[17] Gewa C.A., M. Oguttu, and N.S. Yandell 2012—21. Maternal nutrition in rural Kenya:Heath and socio-demographic determinants and its association with child nutrition. Maternal and child nutrition 8(3); 276-286.

[18] WFP. 2010. Kenya urban comprehensive update and vulnerability analysis (KU-CSFVA) and nutrition assessment (2010), Rome. Found at: www.wfp.org/sites/default/files/urban%20FS%20assessment%20Report_Final.pdf.

[19] Concern Worldwide. 2017. Annual Report, Kenya Country Office, Nairobi.

[20] Kimani-Murage EW, L. Schofield, F. Wekesah, S. Mohamed, B. Mberu, R. Ettarh, T. Egondi, C. Kyobutungi, and A. Ezeh. Vulnerability to Food Insecurity in Urban Slums: Experiences from Nairobi, Kenya. Journal of Urban Health: Bulletin of the New York Academy of Medicine. doi:10.1007/s11524-014-9894-3, 2014.

[21] Kabunga NS, Dubois T, and Qaim M. 2014. Impact of Tissue Culture Banana Technology on Farm Household Income and Food Security in Kenya. 2011. Food Policy **45, January 2011. doi:** 10.1016/j.foodpol.2013.12.009

[22] Jemimah Njuki., Susan Kaaria., Angeline Chamunorwa and Wanjiku Chiuri. 2016**;** Linking Smallholder Farmers to Markets, Gender and Intra-Household Dynamics: Does the Choice of Commodity Matter? European Journal of Development Research April 2011, 23(3):426-443. DOI: 10.1057/ejdr.2011.8,

[23] Lora Iannotti. Dietary Intakes and Micronutrient Adequacy Related to the Changing Livelihoods of Two Pastoralist Communities in Samburu, Kenya. Current Anthropology 55(4):475-482, August 2014, **DOI: 10.1086/677107.**

[24] Haushofer and Shapiro 2016. Policy Brief: Impacts of Unconditional Cash Transfers. October 24, 2016. Advance publication 29th Jul 2016.Quarterly J. Economics. DOI. 10.1093/qje/qjw025.

[25] Merttens F., A. Hurrell., R. Attah., M. Farhat., A. Kardan., and I. MacAuslan. 2013. Kenya Hunger Safety Net Programme (HSNP) Evaluation and Monitoring Component. 2013, Oxford Policy Management Report. June 2013.

[26] OPM and IDS 2012—35. OPM/IDS. HSNP Kenya Monitoring and Evaluation Report Component-analysis and impact final report. Oxford, UK; OPM, Brighton UK, IDS.

[27] Mukuria AG., MT Kothari and N. Abderrahim. 2016. Infant feeding update, ORC Macro, Calverton, Maryland, USA.

[28] FAO. 2002. Independent Evaluation of the Special Programme for Food Security. Rome. found at fao.org/3/y http://www.fao.org/3/y6831e/y6831e.htm#TopOfPage.

[29] Republic of Kenya, Ministry of Health. Kenya Environmental Sanitation and Hygiene Strategic Framework (KESSF), 2016-2020. MoH, Nairobi.

[30] Republic of Kenya, Kenya Gazette Supplement No. 197(Senate Bills No. 12)-Kenya Food Security Bills, 2017. Kenya Senate, Nairobi.

[31] SUN. 2017. Kenya SUN Movement Annual Progress Report 2017. Available at: http://docs.scalingupnutrition.org/wpcontent/uploads/2017/10/Kenya-SUN-Movement-Annual-Progress-Report-2017.pdf.

[32] Commonwealth. 2016. Member Countries-Uganda Economy. Found at: https://www.thecommonwealth.org/our-member-countries/Uganda/economy. Accessed on 15th Apr 2020.

[33] World Bank. 2019. Country Profile-Uganda. Found at: https://data.worldbank.org/country/uganda

[34] UNICEF.2019. Progress for every child in the SDG era-country profile-Uganda. Found at: www.country-profile-Uga.pdf. Accessed 16th Apr 2020.

[35] Nicholson, SE. 1986. The nature of climate variability in Africa south of the Equator. Int. J. Climatology, 6, 515-530. Doi. 10.1002/joc.3370060506. found at: https://www.tandfonline.com/doi/full/10.1080/02626667.2013.804188. Accessed on 16th Apr 2020.

[36] IPC, Uganda. 2014. Uganda Technical IPC working group. 2014. Report of the Integrated food security phase classification Report for Uganda. IPC Tech Working Group, Kampala.

[37] UPPC. 2015. The Public Financial Management Act (2015), Government of Uganda, Entebbe.

[38] World Bank. 2016. Uganda poverty assessment fact sheet: 2016. Found at: https://www.worldbank.org/en/country/uganda/brief/uganda-poverty-assessment-2016-fact-sheet. Accessed 16th Apr 2020.

[39] Republic of Uganda. 2014. The state of Uganda population report 2014-harnessing the demographic dividend for socio-economic growth. Found at: http://npcsec.go.ug/wp-content/uploads/2013/06/State-of-Uganda-Population-Report-2014.pdf. Accessed 16th Apr 2020.

[40] GoU. 2003. Food and Nutrition Policy, 2003, Government of Uganda, Entebbe

[41] GoU. 2010. Poverty (UBOS 2005/2206 FY) and 2008/2009. http://npcsec.go.ug/wp-content/uploads/2013/06/State-of-Uganda-Population-Report-2014.pdf.

[42] USAID. 2010. Food and Technical Assistance Program (FANTA-2); Found at: www.fanta.org.

[43] GAIN. 2017. Fortification Assessment Coverage Tool (FACT) Survey in Uganda. Geneva, Switzerland: GAIN

[44] USAID 2017. "Country Profile: Uganda." Available at: http://www.feedthefuture.gov/country/uganda

[45] World Bank. 2017. "Uganda Country Overview." Available at: http://www.worldbank.org/en/country/uganda/overview

[46] World Bank. 2017. "Tanzania." Available at: http://www.worldbank.org/en/country/tanzania/overview.

[47] World Bank. 2012. Tanzania economic update-spreading the wings. Found at: http://documents.worldbank.org/curated/en/801511468132877390/pdf/733460WP0P133400Box371944B00PUBLIC0.pdf.Accessed on 18th Apr 2020.

[48] WFP 2012. Comprehensive Food Security and Vulnerability Analysis Report, Tanzania, 2012. Found at: https://documents.wfp.org/stellent/groups/public/documents/ena/wfp259830.pdf?iframe. Accessed on 18th Apr 2020.

[49] World Bank. 2011. Economic Growth in Decade 2000-2010. The World Bank in Tanzania, an Overview. Found at: https://www.worldbank.org/en/country/tanzania/overview.

[50] Zanzibar IPC-Zanzibar Food Security and Nutrition Monitoring–IPC Technical Working Group (TWG). 2017. Zanzibar Food Security and Nutrition Analysis Report. August, 2017

[51] United Republic of Tanzania. 2000. The Tanzania Development Vision 2025.

Found at: https://mof.go.tz/mofdocs/overarch/vision2025.htm.Accessed on 10th April 2020.

[52] Statista. 2017. Tanzania-share of economic sectors to GDP from 2007-2017. Found at: https://www.statista.com/statistics/447719/share-of-economic-sectors-in-the-gdp-in-tanzania/. Accessed on 18th Apr 2020.

[53] FAO. 2017. Livestock Brief. Found at: http://www.fao.org/ag/againfo/resources/en/publications/sector_briefs/lsb_TZA.pdf.

[54] Office of the Chief Government Statistician (OCGS) and ICF. 2016. Tanzania Demographic and Health Survey and Malaria Indicator Survey (TDHS-MIS) 2015-16. Dar es Salaam, Tanzania and Rockville, Maryland, USA:

[55] USAID. 2017. "Country Profile: Tanzania." Available at: https://feedthefuture.gov/country/tanzania. Accessed on 12th Apr 2020.